# WHY MEN FIGHT

First Warbler Classics Edition 2023

First published as *Principles of Social Reconstruction* in 1916 by Allen & Unwin, London, and as *Why Men Fight* in the US in 1917 by The Century Co., New York

"The Ethics of War" first published in *The International Journal of Ethics* 25, no. 2 (Jan 1915), 127–142.

Biographical Timeline © 2023 Warbler Press

www.warblerpress.com

ISBN 978-1-962572-78-1 (paperback)
ISBN 978-1-962572-79-8 (e-book)

# WHY MEN FIGHT

## A METHOD OF ABOLISHING
## THE INTERNATIONAL DUEL

# BERTRAND RUSSELL

warbler classics

# CONTENTS

# PREFACE

THE FOLLOWING LECTURES were written in 1915, and delivered in the beginning of 1916 . I had hoped to re-write them considerably, and make them somewhat less inadequate to their theme; but other work, which seemed more pressing, intervened, and the prospect of opportunity for leisurely revision remains remote.

My aim is to suggest a philosophy of politics based upon the belief that impulse has more effect than conscious purpose in moulding men's lives. Most impulses may be divided into two groups, the possessive and the creative, according as they aim at acquiring or retaining something that cannot be shared, or at bringing into the world some valuable thing, such as knowledge or art or goodwill, in which there is no private property. I consider the best life that which is most built on creative impulses, and the worst that which is most inspired by love of possession. Political institutions have a very great influence upon the dispositions of men and women, and should be such as to promote creativeness at the expense of possessiveness. The State, war, and property are the chief political embodiments of the possessive impulses; education, marriage, and religion ought to embody the creative impulses, though at present they do so very inadequately. Liberation of creativeness ought to be the principle of reform both in politics and in economics. It is this conviction which has led to the writing of these lectures.

*September, 1916.*

Le souffle, le rhythme, la vraie force populaire manqua à la réaction. Elle eut les rois, les trésors, les armées; elle écrasa les peuples, mais elle resta muette. Elle tua en silence; elle ne put parler qu'avec le canon sur ses horribles champs de bataille....Tuer quinze millions d'hommes par la faim et l'épée, à la bonne heure, cela se peut. Mais faire un petit chant, un air aimé de tous, voilà ce que nulle machination ne donnera....Don réservé, béni....Ce chant peut-être à l'aube jaillira d'un cœur simple, ou l'alouette le trouvera en montant au soleil, de son sillon d'avril.

—MICHELET

I

# THE PRINCIPLE OF GROWTH

To ALL WHO are capable of new impressions and fresh thought, some modification of former beliefs and hopes has been brought by the war. What the modification has been has depended, in each case, upon character and circumstance; but in one form or another it has been almost universal. To me, the chief thing to be learnt through the war has been a certain view of the springs of human action, what they are, and what we may legitimately hope that they will become. This view, if it is true, seems to afford a basis for political philosophy more capable of standing erect in a time of crisis than the philosophy of traditional Liberalism has shown itself to be. The following lectures, though only one of them will deal with war, all are inspired by a view of the springs of action which has been suggested by the war. And all of them are informed by the hope of seeing such political institutions established in Europe as shall make men averse to war—a hope which I firmly believe to be realizable, though not without a great and fundamental reconstruction of economic and social life.

To one who stands outside the cycle of beliefs and passions which make the war seem necessary, an isolation, an almost unbearable separation from the general activity, becomes unavoidable. At the very moment when the universal disaster raises compassion in the highest degree, compassion itself compels aloofness from the impulse to self-destruction which has swept over Europe. The helpless longing to save men from the ruin towards which they are hastening makes it necessary to oppose the stream, to incur hostility, to be thought unfeeling, to lose for the moment the power of winning belief. It is impossible to prevent others from feeling hostile, but it is possible to avoid any reciprocal hostility on one's own part, by imaginative understanding and the sympathy which grows out of it. And without understanding and sympathy it is impossible to find a cure for the evil from which the world is suffering.

There are two views of the war neither of which seems to me

adequate. The usual view in this country is that it is due to the wickedness of the Germans; the view of most pacifists is that it is due to the diplomatic tangle and to the ambitions of Governments. I think both these views fail to realize the extent to which war grows out of ordinary human nature. Germans, and also the men who compose Governments, are on the whole average human beings, actuated by the same passions that actuate others, not differing much from the rest of the world except in their circumstances. War is accepted by men who are neither Germans nor diplomatists with a readiness, an acquiescence in untrue and inadequate reasons, which would not be possible if any deep repugnance to war were widespread in other nations or classes. The untrue things which men believe, and the true things which they disbelieve, are an index to their impulses—not necessarily to individual impulses in each case (since beliefs are contagious), but to the general impulses of the community. We all believe many things which we have no good ground for believing, because, subconsciously, our nature craves certain kinds of action which these beliefs would render reasonable if they were true. Unfounded beliefs are the homage which impulse pays to reason; and thus it is with the beliefs which, opposite but similar, make men here and in Germany believe it their duty to prosecute the war.

The first thought which naturally occurs to one who accepts this view is that it would be well if men were more under the dominion of reason. War, to those who see that it must necessarily do untold harm to all the combatants, seems a mere madness, a collective insanity in which all that has been known in time of peace is forgotten. If impulses were more controlled, if thought were less dominated by passion, men would guard their minds against the approaches of war fever, and disputes would be adjusted amicably. This is true, but it is not by itself sufficient. It is only those in whom the desire to think truly is itself a passion who will find this desire adequate to control the passions of war. Only passion can control passion, and only a contrary impulse or desire can check impulse. Reason, as it is preached by traditional moralists, is too negative, too little living, to make a good life. It is not by reason alone that wars can be prevented, but by a positive life of impulses and passions antagonistic to those that lead to war. It is the life of impulse that needs to be changed, not only the life of conscious thought.

All human activity springs from two sources: impulse and desire. The part played by desire has always been sufficiently recognized.

When men find themselves not fully contented, and not able instantly to procure what will cause content, imagination brings before their minds the thought of things which they believe would make them happy. All desire involves an interval of time between the consciousness of a need and the opportunity for satisfying it. The acts inspired by desire may be in themselves painful, the time before satisfaction can be achieved may be very long, the object desired may be something outside our own lives, and even after our own death. Will, as a directing force, consists mainly in following desires for more or less distant objects, in spite of the painfulness of the acts involved and the solicitations of incompatible but more immediate desires and impulses. All this is familiar, and political philosophy hitherto has been almost entirely based upon desire as the source of human actions.

But desire governs no more than a part of human activity, and that not the most important but only the more conscious, explicit, and civilized part.

In all the more instinctive part of our nature we are dominated by impulses to certain kinds of activity, not by desires for certain ends. Children run and shout, not because of any good which they expect to realize, but because of a direct impulse to running and shouting. Dogs bay the moon, not because they consider that it is to their advantage to do so, but because they feel an impulse to bark. It is not any purpose, but merely an impulse, that prompts such actions as eating, drinking, love-making, quarreling, boasting. Those who believe that man is a rational animal will say that people boast in order that others may have a good opinion of them; but most of us can recall occasions when we have boasted in spite of knowing that we should be despised for it. Instinctive acts normally achieve some result which is agreeable to the natural man, but they are not performed from desire for this result. They are performed from direct impulse, and the impulse is often strong even in cases in which the normal desirable result cannot follow. Grown men like to imagine themselves more rational than children and dogs, and unconsciously conceal from themselves how great a part impulse plays in their lives. This unconscious concealment always follows a certain general plan. When an impulse is not indulged in the moment in which it arises, there grows up a desire for the expected consequences of indulging the impulse. If some of the consequences which are reasonably to be expected are clearly disagreeable, a conflict between foresight and impulse arises. If the impulse is weak, foresight may conquer; this is what is called acting on reason. If the impulse is strong, either foresight will be falsified, and the disagreeable consequences will be forgotten, or, in men of a heroic mold, the consequences may be recklessly accepted. When Macbeth realizes that he is doomed to defeat, he does not shrink from the fight; he exclaims:—

> Lay on, Macduff,
> And damned be him that first cries, Hold, enough!

But such strength and recklessness of impulse is rare. Most men, when their impulse is strong, succeed in persuading themselves, usually by a subconscious selectiveness of attention, that agreeable consequences will follow from the indulgence of their impulse. Whole philosophies, whole systems of ethical valuation, spring up in this way: they are the embodiment of a kind of thought which is subservient to impulse, which aims at providing a quasi-rational ground for the indulgence of impulse. The only thought which is genuine is that which springs out of the intellectual impulse of curiosity, leading to the desire to know and understand. But most of what passes for thought is inspired by some non-intellectual impulse, and is merely a means of persuading ourselves that we shall not be disappointed or do harm if we indulge this impulse.[1]

When an impulse is restrained, we feel discomfort or even violent pain. We may indulge the impulse in order to escape from this pain, and our action is then one which has a purpose. But the pain only exists because of the impulse, and the impulse itself is directed to an act, not to escaping from the pain of restraining the impulse. The impulse itself remains without a purpose, and the purpose of escaping from pain only arises when the impulse has been momentarily restrained.

Impulse is at the basis of our activity, much more than desire. Desire has its place, but not so large a place as it seemed to have. Impulses bring with them a whole train of subservient fictitious desires: they make men feel that they desire the results which will follow from indulging the impulses, and that they are acting for the sake of these results, when in fact their action has no motive outside itself. A man may write a book or paint a picture under the belief that he desires the praise which it will bring him; but as soon as it is finished, if his creative impulse is not exhausted, what he has done grows uninteresting to him, and he begins a new piece of work. What applies to artistic

---

1    On this subject compare Bernard Hart's "Psychology of Insanity" (Cambridge University Press, 1914), chap. v, especially pp. 62–5.

creation applies equally to all that is most vital in our lives: direct impulse is what moves us, and the desires which we think we have are a mere garment for the impulse.

Desire, as opposed to impulse, has, it is true, a large and increasing share in the regulation of men's lives. Impulse is erratic and anarchical, not easily fitted into a well-regulated system; it may be tolerated in children and artists, but it is not thought proper to men who hope to be taken seriously. Almost all paid work is done from desire, not from impulse: the work itself is more or less irksome, but the payment for it is desired. The serious activities that fill a man's working hours are, except in a few fortunate individuals, governed mainly by purposes, not by impulses towards those activities. In this hardly any one sees an evil, because the place of impulse in a satisfactory existence is not recognized.

An impulse, to one who does not share it actually or imaginatively, will always seem to be mad. All impulse is essentially blind, in the sense that it does not spring from any prevision of consequences. The man who does not share the impulse will form a different estimate as to what the consequences will be, and as to whether those that must ensue are desirable. This difference of opinion will seem to be ethical or intellectual, whereas its real basis is a difference of impulse. No genuine agreement will be reached, in such a case, so long as the difference of impulse persists. In all men who have any vigorous life, there are strong impulses such as may seem utterly unreasonable to others. Blind impulses sometimes lead to destruction and death, but at other times they lead to the best things the world contains. Blind impulse is the source of war, but it is also the source of science, and art, and love. It is not the weakening of impulse that is to be desired, but the direction of impulse towards life and growth rather than towards death and decay.

The complete control of impulse by will, which is sometimes preached by moralists, and often enforced by economic necessity, is not really desirable. A life governed by purposes and desires, to the exclusion of impulse, is a tiring life; it exhausts vitality, and leaves a man, in the end, indifferent to the very purposes which he has been trying to achieve. When a whole nation lives in this way, the whole nation tends to become feeble, without enough grasp to recognize and overcome the obstacles to its desires. Industrialism and organization are constantly forcing civilized nations to live more and more by purpose rather than impulse. In the long run such a mode of existence, if it does not dry up the springs of life, produces new impulses, not of the kind which the will has been in the habit of controlling or of which thought is conscious. These new impulses are apt to be worse in their effects than those that have been checked. Excessive discipline, especially when it is imposed from without, often issues in impulses of cruelty and destruction; this is one reason why militarism has a bad effect on national character. Either lack of vitality, or impulses which are oppressive and against life, will almost always result if the spontaneous impulses are not able to find an outlet. A man's impulses are not fixed from the beginning by his native disposition: within certain wide limits, they are profoundly modified by his circumstances and his way of life. The nature of these modifications ought to be studied, and the results of such study ought to be taken account of in judging the good or harm that is done by political and social institutions.

The war has grown, in the main, out of the life of impulse, not out of reason or desire. There is an impulse of aggression, and an impulse of resistance to aggression. Either may, on occasion, be in accordance with reason, but both are operative in many cases in which they are quite contrary to reason. Each impulse produces a whole harvest of attendant beliefs. The beliefs appropriate to the impulse of aggression may be seen in Bernhardi, or in the early Mohammedan conquerors, or, in full perfection, in the Book of Joshua. There is first of all a conviction of the superior excellence of one's own group, a certainty that they are in some sense the chosen people. This justifies the feeling that only the good and evil of one's own group is of real importance, and that the rest of the world is to be regarded merely as material for the triumph or salvation of the higher race. In modern politics this attitude is embodied in imperialism. Europe as a whole has this attitude towards Asia and Africa, and many Germans have this attitude towards the rest of Europe.

Correlative to the impulse of aggression is the impulse of resistance to aggression. This impulse is exemplified in the attitude of the Israelites to the Philistines or of medieval Europe to the Mohammedans. The beliefs which it produces are beliefs in the peculiar wickedness of those whose aggression is feared, and in the immense value of national customs which they might suppress if they were victorious. When the war broke out, all the reactionaries in England and France began to speak of the danger to democracy, although until that moment they had opposed democracy with all their strength. They were not insincere in so speaking: the impulse of resistance to Germany made them value whatever was endangered by the German attack. They loved democracy because they hated Germany; but they thought they hated Germany because they loved democracy.

The correlative impulses of aggression and resistance to aggression have both been operative in all the countries engaged in the war. Those who have not been dominated by one or other of these impulses may be roughly divided into three classes. There are, first, men whose national sentiment is antagonistic to the State to which they are subject. This class includes some Irish, Poles, Finns, Jews, and other members of oppressed nations. From our point of view, these men may be omitted from our consideration, since they have the same impulsive nature as those who fight, and differ merely in external circumstances.

The second class of men who have not been part of the force supporting the war have been those whose impulsive nature is more or less atrophied. Opponents of pacifism suppose that all pacifists belong to this class, except when they are in German pay. It is thought that pacifists are bloodless, men without passions, men who can look on and reason with cold detachment while their brothers are giving their lives for their country. Among those who are merely passively pacifist, and do no more than abstain from actively taking part in the war, there may be a certain proportion of whom this is true. I think the supporters of war would be right in decrying such men. In spite of all the destruction which is wrought by the impulses that lead to war, there is more hope for a nation which has these impulses than for a nation in which all impulse is dead. Impulse is the expression of life, and while it exists there is hope of its turning towards life instead of towards death; but lack of impulse is death, and out of death no new life will come.

The active pacifists, however, are not of this class: they are not men without impulsive force but men in whom some impulse to which war is hostile is strong enough to overcome the impulses that lead to war. It is not the act of a passionless man to throw himself athwart the whole movement of the national life, to urge an outwardly hopeless cause, to incur obloquy and to resist the contagion of collective emotion. The impulse to avoid the hostility of public opinion is one of the strongest in human nature, and can only be overcome by an unusual force of direct and uncalculating impulse; it is not cold reason alone that can prompt such an act.

Impulses may be divided into those that make for life and those that make for death. The impulses embodied in the war are among those that make for death. Any one of the impulses that make for life, if it is strong enough, will lead a man to stand out against the war. Some of these impulses are only strong in highly civilized men; some are part of common humanity. The impulses towards art and science are among the more civilized of those that make for life. Many artists have remained wholly untouched by the passions of the war, not from feebleness of feeling, but because the creative instinct, the pursuit of a vision, makes them critical of the assaults of national passion, and not responsive to the myth in which the impulse of pugnacity clothes itself. And the few men in whom the scientific impulse is dominant have noticed the rival myths of warring groups, and have been led through understanding to neutrality. But it is not out of such refined impulses that a popular force can be generated which shall be sufficient to transform the world.

There are three forces on the side of life which require no exceptional mental endowment, which are not very rare at present, and might be very common under better social institutions. They are love, the instinct of constructiveness, and the joy of life. All three are checked and enfeebled at present by the conditions under which men live—not only the less outwardly fortunate, but also the majority of the well-to-do. Our institutions rest upon injustice and authority: it is only by closing our hearts against sympathy and our minds against truth that we can endure the oppressions and unfairnesses by which we profit. The conventional conception of what constitutes success leads most men to live a life in which their most vital impulses are sacrificed, and the joy of life is lost in listless weariness. Our economic system compels almost all men to carry out the purposes of others rather than their own, making them feel impotent in action and only able to secure a certain modicum of passive pleasure. All these things destroy the vigor of the community, the expansive affections of individuals, and the power of viewing the world generously. All these things are unnecessary and can be ended by wisdom and courage. If they were ended, the impulsive life of men would become wholly different, and the human race might travel towards a new happiness and a new vigor. To urge this hope is the purpose of these lectures.

The impulses and desires of men and women, in so far as they are of real importance in their lives, are not detached one from another, but proceed from a central principle of growth, an instinctive urgency leading them in a certain direction, as trees seek the light. So long as this instinctive movement is not thwarted, whatever misfortunes may occur are not fundamental disasters, and do not produce those distortions which result from interference with natural growth. This intimate center in each human being is what imagination must apprehend if we are to understand him intuitively. It differs from man to man, and determines for each man the type of excellence of which he is capable. The utmost that social institutions can do for a man is to make his own growth free and vigorous: they cannot force him to grow according to the pattern of another man. There are in men some impulses and desires—for example, those towards drugs—which do not grow out of the central principle; such impulses, when they become strong enough to be harmful, have to be checked by self-discipline. Other impulses, though they may grow out of the central principle in the individual, may be injurious to the growth of others, and they need to be checked in the interest of others. But in the main, the impulses which are injurious to others tend to result from thwarted growth, and to be least in those who have been unimpeded in their instinctive development.

Men, like trees, require for their growth the right soil and a sufficient freedom from oppression. These can be helped or hindered by political institutions. But the soil and the freedom required for a man's growth are immeasurably more difficult to discover and to obtain than the soil and the freedom required for the growth of a tree. And the full growth which may be hoped for cannot be defined or demonstrated; it is subtle and complex, it can only be felt by a delicate intuition and dimly apprehended by imagination and respect. It depends not only or chiefly upon the physical environment, but upon beliefs and affections, upon opportunities for action, and upon the whole life of the community. The more developed and civilized the type of man the more elaborate are the conditions of his growth, and the more dependent they become upon the general state of the society in which he lives. A man's needs and desires are not confined to his own life. If his mind is comprehensive and his imagination vivid, the failures of the community to which he belongs are his failures, and its successes are his successes: according as his community succeeds or fails, his own growth is nourished or impeded.

In the modern world, the principle of growth in most men and women is hampered by institutions inherited from a simpler age. By the progress of thought and knowledge, and by the increase in command over the forces of the physical world, new possibilities of growth have come into existence, and have given rise to new claims which must be satisfied if those who make them are not to be thwarted. There is less acquiescence in limitations which are no longer unavoidable, and less possibility of a good life while those limitations remain. Institutions which give much greater opportunities to some classes than to others are no longer recognized as just by the less fortunate, though the more fortunate still defend them vehemently. Hence arises a universal strife, in which tradition and authority are arrayed against liberty and justice. Our professed morality, being traditional, loses its hold upon those who are in revolt. Coöperation between the defenders of the old and the champions of the new has become almost impossible. An intimate disunion has entered into almost all the relations of life in continually increasing measure. In the fight for freedom, men and women become increasingly unable to break down the walls of the Ego and achieve the growth which comes from a real and vital union.

All our institutions have their historic basis in Authority. The unquestioned authority of the Oriental despot found its religious expression in the omnipotent Creator, whose glory was the sole end of man, and against whom man had no rights. This authority descended to the Emperor and Pope, to the kings of the Middle Ages, to the nobles in the feudal hierarchy, and even to every husband and father in his dealings with his wife and children. The Church was the direct embodiment of the Divine authority, the State and the law were constituted by the authority of the King, private property in land grew out of the authority of conquering barons, and the family was governed by the authority of the pater-familias.

The institutions of the Middle Ages permitted only a fortunate few to develop freely: the vast majority of mankind existed to minister to the few. But so long as authority was genuinely respected and acknowledged even by its least fortunate subjects, medieval society remained organic and not fundamentally hostile to life, since outward submission was compatible with inward freedom because it was voluntary. The institutions of Western Christendom embodied a theory which was really believed, as no theory by which our present institutions can be defended is now believed.

The medieval theory of life broke down through its failure to satisfy men's demands for justice and liberty. Under the stress of oppression, when rulers exceeded their theoretical powers, the victims were forced to realize that they themselves also had rights, and need not live merely to increase the glory of the few. Gradually it came to be seen that if men have power, they are likely to abuse it, and that authority in practice means tyranny. Because the claim to justice was resisted by the holders of power, men became more and more separate units, each fighting for his own rights, not a genuine community bound together by an organic common purpose. This absence of a common purpose has become a source of unhappiness. One of the reasons which led many men to welcome the outbreak of the present war was that it made each nation again a whole community with a single purpose. It did this by destroying, for the present, the beginnings of a single purpose in the civilized world as a whole; but these beginnings were as yet so feeble that few were much affected by their destruction. Men rejoiced in the new sense of unity with their compatriots more than they minded the increased separation from their enemies.

The hardening and separation of the individual in the course of the fight for freedom has been inevitable, and is not likely ever to be wholly undone. What is necessary, if an organic society is to grow up, is that our institutions should be so fundamentally changed as to embody that new respect for the individual and his rights which modern feeling demands. The medieval Empire and Church swept away the individual. There were heretics, but they were massacred relentlessly, without any of the qualms aroused by later persecutions. And they, like their persecutors, were persuaded that there ought to be one universal Church: they differed only as to what its creed should be. Among a few men of art and letters, the Renaissance undermined the medieval theory, without, however, replacing it by anything but skepticism and confusion. The first serious breach in this medieval theory was caused by Luther's assertion of the right of private judgment and the fallibility of General Councils. Out of this assertion grew inevitably, with time, the belief that a man's religion could not be determined for him by authority, but must be left to the free choice of each individual. It was in matters of religion that the battle for liberty began, and it is in matters of religion that it has come nearest to a complete victory.[2]

The development through extreme individualism to strife, and thence, one hopes, to a new reintegration, is to be seen in almost every department of life. Claims are advanced in the name of justice, and resisted in the name of tradition and prescriptive right. Each side honestly believes that it deserves to triumph, because two theories of society exist side by side in our thought, and men choose, unconsciously, the theory which fits their case. Because the battle is long and arduous all general theory is gradually forgotten; in the end, nothing

---

2   This was written before Christianity had become punishable by hard labor, penal servitude, or even death, under the Military Service Act (No. 2). [Note added in 1916.]

remains but self-assertion, and when the oppressed win freedom they are as oppressive as their former masters.

This is seen most crudely in the case of what is called nationalism. Nationalism, in theory, is the doctrine that men, by their sympathies and traditions, form natural groups, called "nations," each of which ought to be united under one central Government. In the main this doctrine may be conceded. But in practice the doctrine takes a more personal form. "I belong," the oppressed nationalist argues, "by sympathy and tradition to nation A, but I am subject to a government which is in the hands of nation B. This is an injustice, not only because of the general principle of nationalism, but because nation A is generous, progressive, and civilized, while nation B is oppressive, retrograde, and barbarous. Because this is so, nation A deserves to prosper, while nation B deserves to be abased." The inhabitants of nation B are naturally deaf to the claims of abstract justice, when they are accompanied by personal hostility and contempt. Presently, however, in the course of war, nation A acquires its freedom. The energy and pride which have achieved freedom generates a momentum which leads on, almost infallibly, to the attempt at foreign conquest, or to the refusal of liberty to some smaller nation. "What? You say that nation C, which forms part of our State, has the same rights against us as we had against nation A? But that is absurd. Nation C is swinish and turbulent, incapable of good government, needing a strong hand if it is not to be a menace and a disturbance to all its neighbors." So the English used to speak of the Irish, so the Germans and Russians speak of the Poles, so the Galician Poles speak of the Ruthenes, so the Austrians used to speak of the Magyars, so the Magyars speak of the South Slav sympathizers with Serbia, so the Serbs speak of the Macedonian Bulgars. In this way nationalism, unobjectionable in theory, leads by a natural movement to oppression and wars of conquest. No sooner was France free from the English, in the fifteenth century, than it embarked upon the conquest of Italy; no sooner was Spain freed from the Moors than it entered into more than a century of conflict with France for the supremacy in Europe. The case of Germany is very interesting in this respect. At the beginning of the eighteenth century German culture was French: French was the language of the Courts, the language in which Leibnitz wrote his philosophy, the universal language of polite letters and learning. National consciousness hardly existed. Then a series of great men created a self-respect in Germany by their achievements in poetry, music, philosophy, and science. But politically German nationalism was only created by Napoleon's oppression and the uprising of 1813. After centuries during which every disturbance of the peace of Europe began with a French or Swedish or Russian invasion of Germany, the Germans discovered that by sufficient effort and union they could keep foreign armies off their territory. But the effort required had been too great to cease when its purely defensive purpose had been achieved by the defeat of Napoleon. Now, a hundred years later, they are still engaged in the same movement, which has become one of aggression and conquest. Whether we are now seeing the end of the movement it is not yet possible to guess.

If men had any strong sense of a community of nations, nationalism would serve to define the boundaries of the various nations. But because men only feel community within their own nation, nothing but force is able to make them respect the rights of other nations, even when they are asserting exactly similar rights on their own behalf.

Analogous development is to be expected, with the course of time, in the conflict between capital and labor which has existed since the growth of the industrial system, and in the conflict between men and women, which is still in its infancy.

What is wanted, in these various conflicts, is some principle, genuinely believed, which will have justice for its outcome. The tug of war of mutual self-assertion can only result in justice through an accidental equality of force. It is no use to attempt any bolstering up of institutions based on authority, since all such institutions involve injustice, and injustice once realized cannot be perpetuated without fundamental damage both to those who uphold it and to those who resist it. The damage consists in the hardening of the walls of the Ego, making them a prison instead of a window. Unimpeded growth in the individual depends upon many contacts with other people, which must be of the nature of free coöperation, not of enforced service. While the belief in authority was alive, free coöperation was compatible with inequality and subjection, but now equality and mutual freedom are necessary. All institutions, if they are not to hamper individual growth, must be based as far as possible upon voluntary combination, rather than the force of the law or the traditional authority of the holders of power. None of our institutions can survive the application of this principle without great and fundamental changes; but these changes are imperatively necessary if the world is to be withheld from dissolving into hard separate units each at war with all the others.

The two chief sources of good relations between individuals are instinctive liking and a common purpose. Of these two, a common purpose might seem more important politically, but, in fact, it is often the outcome, not the cause, of instinctive liking, or of a common instinctive aversion. Biological groups, from the family to the nation, are constituted by a greater or less degree of instinctive liking, and build their common purposes on this foundation.

Instinctive liking is the feeling which makes us take pleasure in another person's company, find an exhilaration in his presence, wish to talk with him, work with him, play with him. The extreme form of it is being in love, but its fainter forms, and even the very faintest, have political importance. The presence of a person who is instinctively disliked tends to make any other person more likable. An anti-Semite will love any fellow-Christian when a Jew is present. In China, or the wilds of Africa, any white man would be welcomed with joy. A common aversion is one of the most frequent causes of mild instinctive liking.

Men differ enormously in the frequency and intensity of their instinctive likings, and the same man will differ greatly at different times. One may take Carlyle and Walt Whitman as opposite poles in this respect. To Carlyle, at any rate in later life, most men and women were repulsive; they inspired an instinctive aversion which made him find pleasure in imagining them under the guillotine or perishing in battle. This led him to belittle most men, finding satisfaction only in those who had been notably destructive of human life—Frederick the Great, Dr. Francia, and Governor Eyre. It led him to love war and violence, and to despise the weak and the oppressed—for example, the "thirty thousand distressed needlewomen," on whom he was never weary of venting his scorn. His morals and his politics, in later life, were inspired through and through by repugnance to almost the whole human race.

Walt Whitman, on the contrary, had a warm, expansive feeling towards the vast majority of men and women. His queer catalogues seemed to him interesting because each item came before his imagination as an object of delight. The sort of joy which most people feel only in those who are exceptionally beautiful or splendid Walt Whitman felt in almost everybody. Out of this universal liking grew optimism, a belief in democracy, and a conviction that it is easy for men to live together in peace and amity. His philosophy and politics, like Carlyle's, were based upon his instinctive attitude towards ordinary men and women.

There is no objective reason to be given to show that one of these attitudes is essentially more rational than the other. If a man finds people repulsive, no argument can prove to him that they are not so. But both his own desires and other people's are much more likely to find satisfaction if he resembles Walt Whitman than if he resembles Carlyle. A world of Walt Whitmans would be happier and more capable of realizing its purposes than a world of Carlyles. For this reason, we shall desire, if we can, to increase the amount of instinctive liking in the world and diminish the amount of instinctive aversion. This is perhaps the most important of all the effects by which political institutions ought to be judged.

The other source of good relations between individuals is a common purpose, especially where that purpose cannot be achieved without knowing its cause. Economic organizations, such as unions and political parties are constituted almost wholly by a common purpose; whatever instinctive liking may come to be associated with them is the result of the common purpose, not its cause. Economic organizations, such as railway companies, subsist for a purpose, but this purpose need only actually exist in those who direct the organization: the ordinary wage-earner need have no purpose beyond earning his wages. This is a defect in economic organizations, and ought to be remedied. One of the objects of syndicalism is to remedy this defect.

Marriage is (or should be) based on instinctive liking, but as soon as there are children, or the wish for children, it acquires the additional strength of a common purpose. It is this chiefly which distinguishes it from an irregular connection not intended to lead to children. Often, in fact, the common purpose survives, and remains a strong tie, after the instinctive liking has faded.

A nation, when it is real and not artificial, is founded upon a faint degree of instinctive liking for compatriots and a common instinctive aversion from foreigners. When an Englishman returns to Dover or Folkestone after being on the Continent, he feels something friendly in the familiar ways: the casual porters, the shouting paper boys, the women serving bad tea, all warm his heart, and seem more "natural," more what human beings ought to be, than the foreigners with their strange habits of behavior. He is ready to believe that all English people are good souls, while many foreigners are full of designing wickedness. It is such feelings that make it easy to organize a nation into a governmental unit. And when that has happened, a common purpose is added, as in marriage. Foreigners would like to invade our country and lay it waste, to kill us in battle, to humble our pride. Those who coöperate with us in preventing this disaster are our friends, and their coöperation intensifies our instinctive liking. But common purposes do not constitute the whole source of our love of country: allies, even of long standing, do not call out the same feelings as are called out by our compatriots. Instinctive liking, resulting largely from similar habits and customs, is an essential element in patriotism, and, indeed, the foundation upon which the whole feeling rests.

If men's natural growth is to be promoted and not hindered by the environment, if as many as possible of their desires and needs are to be satisfied, political institutions must, as far as possible, embody common purposes and foster instinctive liking. These two objects are interconnected, for nothing is so destructive of instinctive liking as thwarted purposes and unsatisfied needs, and nothing facilitates coöperation for common purposes so much as instinctive liking. When a man's growth is unimpeded, his self-respect remains intact, and he is not inclined to regard others as his enemies. But when, for whatever reason, his growth is impeded, or he is compelled to grow into some twisted and unnatural shape, his instinct presents the environment as his enemy, and he becomes filled with hatred. The joy of life abandons him, and malevolence takes the place of friendliness. The malevolence of hunchbacks and cripples is proverbial; and a similar malevolence is to be found in those who have been crippled in less obvious ways. Real freedom, if it could be brought about, would go a long way towards destroying hatred.

There is a not uncommon belief that what is instinctive in us cannot be changed, but must be simply accepted and made the best of. This is by no means the case. No doubt we have a certain native disposition, different in different people, which coöperates with outside circumstances in producing a certain character. But even the instinctive part of our character is very malleable. It may be changed by beliefs, by material circumstances, by social circumstances, and by institutions. A Dutchman has probably much the same native disposition as a German, but his instincts in adult life are very different owing to the absence of militarism and of the pride of a Great Power. It is obvious that the instincts of celibates become profoundly different from those of other men and women. Almost any instinct is capable of many different forms according to the nature of the outlets which it finds. The same instinct which leads to artistic or intellectual creativeness may, under other circumstances, lead to love of war. The fact that an activity or belief is an outcome of instinct is therefore no reason for regarding it as unalterable.

This applies to people's instinctive likes and dislikes as well as to their other instincts. It is natural to men, as to other animals, to like some of their species and dislike others; but the proportion of like and dislike depends on circumstances, often on quite trivial circumstances. Most of Carlyle's misanthropy is attributable to dyspepsia; probably a suitable medical regimen would have given him a completely different outlook on the world. The defect of punishment, as a means of dealing with impulses which the community wishes to discourage, is that it does nothing to prevent the existence of the impulses, but merely endeavors to check their indulgence by an appeal to self-interest. This method, since it does not eradicate the impulses, probably only drives them to find other outlets even when it is successful in its immediate object; and if the impulses are strong, mere self-interest is not likely to curb them effectually, since it is not a very powerful motive except with unusually reasonable and rather passionless people. It is thought to be a stronger motive than it is, because our moods make us deceive ourselves as to our interest, and lead us to believe that it is consistent with the actions to which we are prompted by desire or impulse.

Thus the commonplace that human nature cannot be changed is untrue. We all know that our own characters and those of our acquaintance are greatly affected by circumstances; and what is true of individuals is true also of nations. The root causes of changes in average human nature are generally either purely material changes—for instance, of climate—or changes in the degree of man's control over the material world. We may ignore the purely material changes, since these do not much concern the politician. But the changes due to man's increased control over the material world, by inventions and science, are of profound present importance. Through the industrial revolution, they have radically altered the daily lives of men; and by creating huge economic organizations, they have altered the whole structure of society. The general beliefs of men, which are, in the main, a product of instinct and circumstance, have become very different from what they were in the eighteenth century. But our institutions are not yet suited either to the instincts developed by our new circumstances, or to our real beliefs. Institutions have a life of their own, and often outlast the circumstances which made them a fit garment for instinct. This applies, in varying degrees, to almost all the institutions which we have inherited from the past: the State, private property, the patriarchal family, the Churches, armies and navies. All of these have become in some degree oppressive, in some measures hostile to life.

In any serious attempt at political reconstruction, it is necessary to realize what are the vital needs of ordinary men and women. It is customary, in political thought, to assume that the only needs with which politics is concerned are economic needs. This view is quite inadequate to account for such an event as the present war, since any economic motives that may be assigned for it are to a great extent mythical, and its true causes must be sought for outside the economic sphere. Needs which are normally satisfied without conscious effort remain unrecognized, and this results in a working theory of human needs which is far too simple. Owing chiefly to industrialism, many needs which were formerly satisfied without effort now remain unsatisfied in most men and women. But the old unduly simple theory of human needs survives, making men overlook the source of the new lack of satisfaction, and invent quite false theories as to why they are dissatisfied. Socialism as a panacea seems to me to be mistaken in this way, since it is too ready to suppose that better economic conditions will of themselves make men happy. It is not only more material goods that men need, but more freedom, more self-direction, more outlet for creativeness, more opportunity for the joy of life, more voluntary coöperation, and less involuntary subservience to purposes not their own. All these things the institutions of the future must help to produce, if our increase of knowledge and power over Nature is to bear its full fruit in bringing about a good life.

## II

# THE STATE

U NDER THE INFLUENCE of socialism, most liberal thought in recent years has been in favor of increasing the power of the State, but more or less hostile to the power of private property. On the other hand, syndicalism has been hostile both to the State and to private property. I believe that syndicalism is more nearly right than socialism in this respect, that both private property and the State, which are the two most powerful institutions of the modern world, have become harmful to life through excess of power, and that both are hastening the loss of vitality from which the civilized world increasingly suffers. The two institutions are closely connected, but for the present I wish to consider only the State. I shall try to show how great, how unnecessary, how harmful, many of its powers are, and how enormously they might be diminished without loss of what is useful in its activity. But I shall admit that in certain directions its functions ought to be extended rather than curtailed.

Some of the functions of the State, such as the Post Office and elementary education, might be performed by private agencies, and are only undertaken by the State from motives of convenience. But other matters, such as the law, the police, the Army, and the Navy, belong more essentially to the State: so long as there is a State at all it is difficult to imagine these matters in private hands. The distinction between socialism and individualism turns on the nonessential functions of the State, which the socialist wishes to extend and the individualist to restrict. It is the essential functions, which are admitted by individualists and socialists alike, that I wish to criticize, since the others do not appear to me in themselves objectionable.

The essence of the State is that it is the repository of the collective force of its citizens. This force takes two forms, one internal and one external. The internal form is the law and the police; the external form is the power of waging war, as embodied in the Army and Navy. The State is constituted by the combination of all the inhabitants in a certain area using their united force in accordance with the commands of a Government. In a civilized State force is only employed against its own citizens in accordance with rules previously laid down, which constitute the criminal law. But the employment of force against foreigners is not regulated by any code of rules, and proceeds, with few exceptions, according to some real or fancied national interest.

There can be no doubt that force employed according to law is less pernicious than force employed capriciously. If international law could acquire sufficient hold on men's allegiance to regulate the relations of States, a very great advance on our present condition would have been made. The primitive anarchy which precedes law is worse than law. But I believe there is a possibility of a stage to some extent above law, where the advantages now secured by the law are secured without loss of freedom, and without the disadvantages which the law and the police render inevitable. Probably some repository of force in the background will remain necessary, but the actual employment of force may become very rare, and the degree of force required very small. The anarchy which precedes law gives freedom only to the strong; the condition to be aimed at will give freedom as nearly as possible to every one. It will do this, not by preventing altogether the existence of organized force, but by limiting the occasions for its employment to the greatest possible extent.

The power of the State is only limited internally by the fear of rebellion and externally by the fear of defeat in war. Subject to these restrictions, it is absolute. In practice, it can seize men's property through taxation, determine the law of marriage and inheritance, punish the expression of opinions which it dislikes, put men to death for wishing the region they inhabit to belong to a different State, and order all able-bodied males to risk their lives in battle whenever it considers war desirable. On many matters disagreement with the purposes and opinions of the State is criminal. Probably the freest States in the world, before the war, were America and England; yet in America no immigrant may land until he has professed disbelief in anarchism and polygamy, while in England men were sent to prison in recent years for expressing disagreement with the Christian religion[1] or agreement with the teaching of Christ.[2] In time of war, all criticism of the external policy of the State is criminal. Certain objects having appeared

---

1    The blasphemy prosecutions.
2    The syndicalist prosecutions. [The punishment of conscientious objectors must now be added, 1916.]

desirable to the majority, or to the effective holders of power, those who do not consider these objects desirable are exposed to pains and penalties not unlike those suffered by heretics in the past. The extent of the tyranny thus exercised is concealed by its very success: few men consider it worth while to incur a persecution which is almost certain to be thorough and effective.

Universal military service is perhaps the extreme example of the power of the State, and the supreme illustration of the difference between its attitude to its own citizens and its attitude to the citizens of other States. The State punishes, with impartial rigor, both those who kill their compatriots and those who refuse to kill foreigners. On the whole, the latter is considered the graver crime. The phenomenon of war is familiar, and men fail to realize its strangeness; to those who stand inside the cycle of instincts which lead to war it all seems natural and reasonable. But to those who stand outside the strangeness of it grows with familiarity. It is amazing that the vast majority of men should tolerate a system which compels them to submit to all the horrors of the battlefield at any moment when their Government commands them to do so. A French artist, indifferent to politics, attentive only to his painting, suddenly finds himself called upon to shoot Germans, who, his friends assure him, are a disgrace to the human race. A German musician, equally unknowing, is called upon to shoot the perfidious Frenchman. Why cannot the two men declare a mutual neutrality? Why not leave war to those who like it and bring it on? Yet if the two men declared a mutual neutrality they would be shot by their compatriots. To avoid this fate they try to shoot each other. If the world loses the artist, not the musician, Germany rejoices; if the world loses the musician, not the artist, France rejoices. No one remembers the loss to civilization, which is equal whichever is killed.

This is the politics of Bedlam. If the artist and the musician had been allowed to stand aside from the war, nothing but unmitigated good to mankind would have resulted. The power of the State, which makes this impossible, is a wholly evil thing, quite as evil as the power of the Church which in former days put men to death for unorthodox thought. Yet if, even in time of peace, an international league were founded to consist of Frenchmen and Germans in equal numbers, all pledged not to take part in war, the French State and the German State would persecute it with equal ferocity. Blind obedience, unlimited willingness to kill and die are exacted of the modern citizens of a democracy as much as of the Janizaries of medieval sultans or the secret agents of Oriental despots.[3]

The power of the State may be brought to bear, as it often is in England, through public opinion rather than through the laws. By oratory and the influence of the Press, public opinion is largely created by the State, and a tyrannous public opinion is as great an enemy to liberty as tyrannous laws. If the young man who will not fight finds that he is dismissed from his employment, insulted in the streets, cold-shouldered by his friends, and thrown over with scorn by any woman who may formerly have liked him, he will feel the penalty quite as hard to bear as a death sentence.[4] A free community requires not only legal freedom, but a tolerant public opinion, an absence of that instinctive inquisition into our neighbors' affairs which, under the guise of upholding a high moral standard, enables good people to indulge unconsciously a disposition to cruelty and persecution. Thinking ill of others is not in itself a good reason for thinking well of ourselves. But so long as this is not recognized, and so long as the State can manufacture public opinion, except in the rare cases where it is revolutionary, public opinion must be reckoned as a definite part of the power of the State.

The power of the State outside its own borders is in the main derived from war or the threat of war. Some power is derived from the ability

---

3   In a democratic country it is the majority who must after all rule, and the minority will be obliged to submit with the best grace possible (*Westminster Gazette* on Conscription, December 29, 1915).

4   Some very strong remarks on the conduct of the "white feather" women were made by Mr. Reginald Kemp, the Deputy Coroner for West Middlesex, at an inquest at Ealing on Saturday on Richard Charles Roberts, aged thirty-four, a taxicab driver, of Shepherd's Bush, who committed suicide in consequence of worry caused by his rejection from the Army and the taunts of women and other amateur recruiters.

It was stated that he tried to join the Army in October, but was rejected on account of a weak heart. That alone, said his widow, had depressed him, and he had been worried because he thought he would lose his license owing to the state of his heart. He had also been troubled by the dangerous illness of a child.

A soldier relative said that the deceased's life had been made "a perfect misery" by women who taunted him and called him a coward because he did not join the Army. A few days ago two women in Maida Vale insulted him "something shocking."

The Coroner, speaking with some warmth, said the conduct of such women was abominable. It was scandalous that women who knew nothing of individual circumstances should be allowed to go about making unbearable the lives of men who had tried to do their duty. It was a pity they had nothing better to do. Here was a man who perhaps had been driven to death by a pack of silly women. He hoped something would soon be done to put a stop to such conduct (*Daily News*, July 26, 1915).

to persuade its citizens to lend money or not to lend it, but this is unimportant in comparison with the power derived from armies and navies. The external activity of the State—with exceptions so rare as to be negligible—is selfish. Sometimes selfishness is mitigated by the need of retaining the goodwill of other States, but this only modifies the methods employed, not the ends pursued. The ends pursued, apart from mere defense against other States, are, on the one hand, opportunities for successful exploitation of weak or uncivilized countries, on the other hand, power and prestige, which are considered more glorious and less material than money. In pursuit of these objects, no State hesitates to put to death innumerable foreigners whose happiness is not compatible with exploitation or subjection, or to devastate territories into which it is thought necessary to strike terror. Apart from the present war, such acts have been performed within the last twenty years by many minor States and by all the Great Powers[5] except Austria; and in the case of Austria only the opportunity, not the will, was lacking.

Why do men acquiesce in the power of the State? There are many reasons, some traditional, some very present and pressing.

The traditional reason for obedience to the State is personal loyalty to the sovereign. European States grew up under the feudal system, and were originally the several territories owned by feudal chiefs. But this source of obedience has decayed, and probably now counts for little except in Japan, and to a lesser extent in Russia.

Tribal feeling, which always underlay loyalty to the sovereign, has remained as strong as it ever was, and is now the chief support for the power of the State. Almost every man finds it essential to his happiness to feel himself a member of a group, animated by common friendships and enmities and banded together for defense and attack. But such groups are of two kinds: there are those which are essentially enlargements of the family, and there are those which are based upon a conscious common purpose. Nations belong to the first kind, Churches to the second. At times when men are profoundly swayed by creeds national divisions tend to break down, as they did in the wars of religion after the Reformation. At such times a common creed is a stronger bond than a common nationality. To a much slighter extent, the same thing has occurred in the modern world with the rise of

---

5    By England in South Africa, America in the Philippines, France in Morocco, Italy in Tripoli, Germany in Southwest Africa, Russia in Persia and Manchuria, Japan in Manchuria.

socialism. Men who disbelieve in private property, and feel the capitalist the real enemy, have a bond which transcends national divisions. It has not been found strong enough to resist the passions aroused by the present war, but it has made them less bitter among socialists than among others, and has kept alive the hope of a European community to be reconstructed when the war is over. In the main, however, the universal disbelief in creeds has left tribal feeling triumphant, and has made nationalism stronger than at any previous period of the world's history. A few sincere Christians, a few sincere socialists, have found in their creed a force capable of resisting the assaults of national passion, but they have been too few to influence the course of events or even to cause serious anxiety to the Governments.

It is chiefly tribal feeling that generates the unity of a national State, but it is not only tribal feeling that generates its strength. Its strength results principally from two fears, neither of which is unreasonable: the fear of crime and anarchy within, and the fear of aggression from without.

The internal orderliness of a civilized community is a great achievement, chiefly brought about by the increased authority of the State. It would be inconvenient if peaceable citizens were constantly in imminent risk of being robbed and murdered. Civilized life would become almost impossible if adventurous people could organize private armies for purposes of plunder. These conditions existed in the Middle Ages, and have not passed away without a great struggle. It is thought by many—especially by the rich, who derive the greatest advantage from law and order—that any diminution in the power of the State might bring back a condition of universal anarchy. They regard strikes as portents of dissolution. They are terrified by such organizations as the Confédération Générale du Travail and the International Workers of the World. They remember the French Revolution, and feel a not unnatural desire to keep their heads on their shoulders. They dread particularly any political theory which seems to excuse private crimes, such as sabotage and political assassination. Against these dangers they see no protection except the maintenance of the authority of the State, and the belief that all resistance to the State is wicked.

Fear of the danger within is enhanced by fear of the danger without. Every State is exposed at all times to the risk of foreign invasion. No means has hitherto been devised for minimizing this risk except the increase of armaments. But the armaments which are nominally intended to repel invasion may also be used to invade. And so the means adopted to diminish the external fear have the effect of increasing it, and of enormously enhancing the destructiveness of war when it does break out. In this way a reign of terror becomes universal, and the State acquires everywhere something of the character of the Comité du Salut Public.

The tribal feeling out of which the State develops is natural, and the fear by which the State is strengthened is reasonable under present circumstances. And in addition to these two, there is a third source of strength in a national State, namely patriotism in its religious aspect.

Patriotism is a very complex feeling, built up out of primitive instincts and highly intellectual convictions. There is love of home and family and friends, making us peculiarly anxious to preserve our own country from invasion. There is the mild instinctive liking for compatriots as against foreigners. There is pride, which is bound up with the success of the community to which we feel that we belong. There is a belief, suggested by pride but reinforced by history, that one's own nation represents a great tradition and stands for ideals that are important to the human race. But besides all these, there is another element, at once nobler and more open to attack, an element of worship, of willing sacrifice, of joyful merging of the individual life in the life of the nation. This religious element in patriotism is essential to the strength of the State, since it enlists the best that is in most men on the side of national sacrifice.

The religious element in patriotism is reinforced by education, especially by a knowledge of the history and literature of one's own country, provided it is not accompanied by much knowledge of the history and literature of other countries. In every civilized country all instruction of the young emphasizes the merits of their own nation and the faults of other nations. It comes to be universally believed that one's own nation, because of its superiority, deserves support in a quarrel, however the quarrel may have originated. This belief is so genuine and deep that it makes men endure patiently, almost gladly, the losses and hardships and sufferings entailed by war. Like all sincerely believed religions, it gives an outlook on life, based upon instinct but sublimating it, causing a devotion to an end greater than any personal end, but containing many personal ends as it were in solution.

Patriotism as a religion is unsatisfactory because of its lack of universality. The good at which it aims is a good for one's own nation only, not for all mankind. The desires which it inspires in an Englishman are not the same as the desires which it inspires in a German. A world full of patriots may be a world full of strife. The more intensely a nation believes in its patriotism, the more fanatically indifferent it will become to the damage suffered by other nations. When once men have learnt to subordinate their own good to the good of a larger whole, there can be no valid reason for stopping short of the human race. It is the admixture of national pride that makes it so easy in practice for men's impulses towards sacrifice to stop short at the frontiers of their own country. It is this admixture that poisons patriotism, and makes it inferior, as a religion, to beliefs which aim at the salvation of all mankind. We cannot avoid having more love for our own country than for other countries, and there is no reason why we should wish to avoid it, any more than we should wish to love all individual men and women equally. But any adequate religion will lead us to temper inequality of affection by love of justice, and to universalize our aims by realizing the common needs of man. This change was effected by Christianity in Judaism, and must be effected in any merely national religion before it can be purged of evil.

In practice, patriotism has many other enemies to contend with. Cosmopolitanism cannot fail to grow as men acquire more knowledge of foreign countries by education and travel. There is also a kind of individualism which is continually increasing, a realization that every man ought to be as nearly free as possible to choose his own ends, not compelled by a geographical accident to pursue ends forced upon him by the community. Socialism, syndicalism, and anti-capitalist movements generally, are against patriotism in their tendency, since they make men aware that the present State is largely concerned in defending the privileges of the rich, and that many of the conflicts between States have their origin in the financial interests of a few plutocrats. This kind of opposition is perhaps temporary, a mere incident in the struggle of labor to acquire power. Australia, where labor feels its triumph secure, is full of patriotism and militarism, based upon determination to prevent foreign labor from sharing the benefits of a privileged position. It is not unlikely that England might develop a similar nationalism if it became a socialist State. But it is probable that such nationalism would be purely defensive. Schemes of foreign aggression, entailing great loss of life and wealth in the nation which adopts them, would hardly be initiated except by those whose instincts of dominion have been sharpened through the power derived from private property and the institutions of the capitalist State.

The evil wrought in the modern world by the excessive power of the

State is very great, and very little recognized.

The chief harm wrought by the State is promotion of efficiency in war. If all States increase their strength, the balance of power is unchanged, and no one State has a better chance of victory than before. And when the means of offense exist, even though their original purpose may have been defensive, the temptation to use them is likely, sooner or later, to prove overwhelming. In this way the very measures which promoted security within the borders of the State promote insecurity elsewhere. It is of the essence of the State to suppress violence within and to facilitate it without. The State makes an entirely artificial division of mankind and of our duties toward them: towards one group we are bound by the law, towards the other only by the prudence of highwaymen. The State is rendered evil by its exclusions, and by the fact that, whenever it embarks upon aggressive war, it becomes a combination of men for murder and robbery. The present system is irrational, since external and internal anarchy must be both right or both wrong. It is supported because, so long as others adopt it, it is thought the only road to safety, and because it secures the pleasures of triumph and dominion, which cannot be obtained in a good community. If these pleasures were no longer sought, or no longer possible to obtain, the problem of securing safety from invasion would not be difficult.

Apart from war, the modern great State is harmful from its vastness and the resulting sense of individual helplessness. The citizen who is out of sympathy with the aims of the State, unless he is a man of very rare gifts, cannot hope to persuade the State to adopt purposes which seem to him better. Even in a democracy, all questions except a very few are decided by a small number of officials and eminent men; and even the few questions which are left to the popular vote are decided by a diffused mass-psychology, not by individual initiative. This is especially noticeable in a country like the United States, where, in spite of democracy, most men have a sense of almost complete impotence in regard to all large issues. In so vast a country the popular will is like one of the forces of Nature, and seems nearly as much outside the control of any one man. This state of things leads, not only in America but in all large States, to something of the weariness and discouragement that we associate with the Roman Empire. Modern States, as opposed to the small city States of ancient Greece or medieval Italy, leave little room for initiative, and fail to develop in most men any sense of ability to control their political destinies. The few men who achieve power in such States are men of abnormal ambition and thirst for dominion, combined with skill in cajolery and subtlety in negotiation. All the rest are dwarfed by knowledge of their own impotence.

A curious survival from the old monarchical idea of the State is the belief that there is some peculiar wickedness in a wish to secede on the part of any section of the population. If Ireland or Poland desires independence, it is thought obvious that this desire must be strenuously resisted, and any attempt to secure it is condemned as "high treason." The only instance to the contrary that I can remember is the separation of Norway and Sweden, which was commended but not imitated. In other cases, nothing but defeat in war has induced States to part with territory: although this attitude is taken for granted, it is not one which would be adopted if the State had better ends in view. The reason for its adoption is that the chief end of almost all great States is power, especially power in war. And power in war is often increased by the inclusion of unwilling citizens. If the well-being of the citizens were the end in view, the question whether a certain area should be included, or should form a separate State, would be left freely to the decision of that area. If this principle were adopted, one of the main reasons for war would be obviated, and one of the most tyrannical elements in the State would be removed.

The principal source of the harm done by the State is the fact that power is its chief end. This is not the case in America, because America is safe against aggression;[6] but in all other great nations the chief aim of the State is to possess the greatest possible amount of external force. To this end, the liberty of the citizens is curtailed, and anti-militarist propaganda is severely punished. This attitude is rooted in pride and fear: pride, which refuses to be conciliatory, and fear, which dreads the results of foreign pride conflicting with our own pride. It seems something of a historical accident that these two passions, which by no means exhaust the political passions of the ordinary man, should so completely determine the external policy of the State. Without pride, there would be no occasion for fear: fear on the part of one nation is due to the supposed pride of another nation. Pride of dominion, unwillingness to decide disputes otherwise than by force or the threat of force, is a habit of mind greatly encouraged by the possession of power. Those who have long been in the habit of exercising power become autocratic and quarrelsome, incapable of regarding an equal otherwise than as a rival. It is notorious that head masters' conferences are more liable to violent disagreements than most similar bodies: each head master tries

6    This was written in 1915.

to treat the others as he treats his own boys; they resent such treatment, and he resents their resentment. Men who have the habit of authority are peculiarly unfit for friendly negotiation; but the official relations of States are mainly in the hands of men with a great deal of authority in their own country. This is, of course, more particularly the case where there is a monarch who actually governs. If is less true where there is a governing oligarchy, and still less true where there is some approach to real democracy. But it is true to a considerable extent in all countries, because Prime Ministers and Foreign Secretaries are necessarily men in authority. The first step towards remedying this state of things is a genuine interest in foreign affairs on the part of the ordinary citizen, and an insistence that national pride shall not be allowed to jeopardize his other interests. During war, when he is roused, he is willing to sacrifice everything to pride; but in quiet times he will be far more ready than men in authority to realize that foreign affairs, like private concerns, ought to be settled amicably according to principles, not brutally by force or the threat of force.

The effect of personal bias in the men who actually compose the Government may be seen very clearly in labor disputes. French syndicalists affirm that the State is simply a product of capitalism, a part of the weapons which capital employs in its conflict with labor. Even in democratic States there is much to bear out this view. In strikes it is common to order out the soldiers to coerce the strikers; although the employers are much fewer, and much easier to coerce, the soldiers are never employed against them. When labor troubles paralyze the industry of a country, it is the men who are thought to be unpatriotic, not the masters, though clearly the responsibility belongs to both sides. The chief reason for this attitude on the part of Governments is that the men composing them belong, by their success if not by their origin, to the same class as the great employers of labor. Their bias and their associates combine to make them view strikes and lockouts from the standpoint of the rich. In a democracy public opinion and the need of conciliating political supporters partially correct these plutocratic influences, but the correction is always only partial. And the same influences which warp the views of Governments on labor questions also warp their views on foreign affairs, with the added disadvantage that the ordinary citizen has much fewer means of arriving at an independent judgment.

The excessive power of the State, partly through internal oppression, but principally through war and the fear of war, is one of the chief causes of misery in the modern world, and one of the main reasons for the discouragement which prevents men from growing to their full mental stature. Some means of curing this excessive power must be found if men are not to be organized into despair, as they were in the Roman Empire.

The State has one purpose which is on the whole good, namely, the substitution of law for force in the relations of men. But this purpose can only be fully achieved by a world-State, without which international relations cannot be made subject to law. And although law is better than force, law is still not the best way of settling disputes. Law is too static, too much on the side of what is decaying, too little on the side of what is growing. So long as law is in theory supreme, it will have to be tempered, from time to time, by internal revolution and external war. These can only be prevented by perpetual readiness to alter the law in accordance with the present balance of forces. If this is not done, the motives for appealing to force will sooner or later become irresistible. A world-State or federation of States, if it is to be successful, will have to decide questions, not by the legal maxims which would be applied by the Hague tribunal, but as far as possible in the same sense in which they would be decided by war. The function of authority should be to render the appeal to force unnecessary, not to give decisions contrary to those which would be reached by force.

This view may be thought by some to be immoral. It may be said that the object of civilization should be to secure justice, not to give the victory to the strong. But when this antithesis is allowed to pass, it is forgotten that love of justice may itself set force in motion. A Legislature which wishes to decide an issue in the same way as it would be decided if there were an appeal to force will necessarily take account of justice, provided justice is so flagrantly on one side that disinterested parties are willing to take up the quarrel. If a strong man assaults a weak man in the streets of London, the balance of force is on the side of the weak man, because, even if the police did not appear, casual passers-by would step in to defend him. It is sheer cant to speak of a contest of might against right, and at the same time to hope for a victory of the right. If the contest is really between might and right, that *means* that right will be beaten. What is obscurely intended, when this phrase is used, is that the stronger side is only rendered stronger by men's sense of right. But men's sense of right is very subjective, and is only one factor in deciding the preponderance of force. What is desirable in a Legislature is, not that it should decide by its personal sense of right, but that it should decide in a way which is felt to make an appeal to force unnecessary.

Having considered what the State ought not to do, I come now to what it ought to do.

Apart from war and the preservation of internal order, there are certain more positive functions which the State performs, and certain others which it ought to perform.

We may lay down two principles as regards these positive functions.

First: there are matters in which the welfare of the whole community depends upon the practically universal attainment of a certain minimum; in such cases the State has the right to insist upon this minimum being attained.

Secondly: there are ways in which, by insisting upon the maintenance of law, the State, if it does nothing further, renders possible various forms of injustice which would otherwise be prevented by the anger of their victims. Such injustices ought, as far as possible, to be prevented by the State.

The most obvious example of a matter where the general welfare depends upon a universal minimum is sanitation and the prevention of infectious diseases. A single case of plague, if it is neglected, may cause disaster to a whole community. No one can reasonably maintain, on general grounds of liberty, that a man suffering from plague ought to be left free to spread infection far and wide. Exactly similar considerations apply to drainage, notification of fevers, and kindred matters. The interference with liberty remains an evil, but in some cases it is clearly a smaller evil than the spread of disease which liberty would produce. The stamping out of malaria and yellow fever by destroying mosquitoes is perhaps the most striking example of the good which can be done in this way. But when the good is small or doubtful, and the interference with liberty is great, it becomes better to endure a certain amount of preventable disease rather than suffer a scientific tyranny.

Compulsory education comes under the same head as sanitation. The existence of ignorant masses in a population is a danger to the community; when a considerable percentage are illiterate, the whole machinery of government has to take account of the fact. Democracy in its modern form would be quite impossible in a nation where many men cannot read. But in this case there is not the same need of absolute universality as in the case of sanitary measures. The gipsies, whose mode of life has been rendered almost impossible by the education authorities, might well have been allowed to remain a picturesque exception. But apart from such rather unimportant exceptions, the argument for compulsory education is irresistible.

What the State does for the care of children at present is less than what ought to be done, not more. Children are not capable of looking after their own interests, and parental responsibility is in many ways inadequate. It is clear that the State alone can insist upon the children being provided with the minimum of knowledge and health which, for the time being, satisfies the conscience of the community.

The encouragement of scientific research is another matter which comes rightly within the powers of the State, because the benefits of discoveries accrue to the community, while the investigations are expensive and never individually certain of achieving any result. In this matter, Great Britain lags behind all other civilized countries.

The second kind of powers which the State ought to possess are those that aim at diminishing economic injustice. It is this kind that has been emphasized by socialists. The law creates or facilitates monopolies, and monopolies are able to exact a toll from the community. The most glaring example is the private ownership of land. Railways are at present controlled by the State, since rates are fixed by law; and it is clear that if they were uncontrolled, they would acquire a dangerous degree of power.[7] Such considerations, if they stood alone, would justify complete socialism. But I think justice, by itself, is, like law, too static to be made a supreme political principle: it does not, when it has been achieved, contain any seeds of new life or any impetus to development. For this reason, when we wish to remedy an injustice, it is important to consider whether, in so doing, we shall be destroying the incentive to some form of vigorous action which is on the whole useful to the community. No such form of action, so far as I can see, is associated with private ownership of land or of any other source of economic rent; if this is the case, it follows that the State ought to be the primary recipient of rent.

If all these powers are allowed to the State, what becomes of the attempt to rescue individual liberty from its tyranny?

This is part of the general problem which confronts all those who still care for the ideals which inspired liberalism, namely the problem of combining liberty and personal initiative with organization. Politics and economics are more and more dominated by vast organizations, in face of which the individual is in danger of becoming powerless.

---

7    This would be as true under a syndicalist régime as it is at present.

The State is the greatest of these organizations, and the most serious menace to liberty. And yet it seems that many of its functions must be extended rather than curtailed.

There is one way by which organization and liberty can be combined, and that is, by securing power for voluntary organizations, consisting of men who have chosen to belong to them because they embody some purpose which all their members consider important, not a purpose imposed by accident or outside force. The State, being geographical, cannot be a wholly voluntary association, but for that very reason there is need of a strong public opinion to restrain it from a tyrannical use of its powers. This public opinion, in most matters, can only be secured by combinations of those who have certain interests or desires in common.

The positive purposes of the State, over and above the preservation of order, ought as far as possible to be carried out, not by the State itself, but by independent organizations, which should be left completely free so long as they satisfied the State that they were not falling below a necessary minimum. This occurs to a certain limited extent at present in regard to elementary education. The universities, also, may be regarded as acting for the State in the matter of higher education and research, except that in their case no minimum of achievement is exacted. In the economic sphere, the State ought to exercise control, but ought to leave initiative to others. There is every reason to multiply opportunities of initiative, and to give the greatest possible share of initiative to each individual, for if this is not done there will be a general sense of impotence and discouragement. There ought to be a constant endeavor to leave the more positive aspects of government in the hands of voluntary organizations, the purpose of the State being merely to exact efficiency and to secure an amicable settlement of disputes, whether within or without its own borders. And with this ought to be combined the greatest possible toleration of exceptions and the least possible insistence upon uniform system.

A good deal may be achieved through local government by trades as well as by areas. This is the most original idea in syndicalism, and it is valuable as a check upon the tyranny which the community may be tempted to exercise over certain classes of its members. All strong organizations which embody a sectional public opinion, such as trade unions, coöperative societies, professions, and universities, are to be welcomed as safeguards of liberty and opportunities for initiative. And there is need of a strong public opinion in favor of liberty itself. The old battles for freedom of thought and freedom of speech, which it was thought had been definitively won, will have to be fought all over again, since most men are only willing to accord freedom to opinions which happen to be popular. Institutions cannot preserve liberty unless men realize that liberty is precious and are willing to exert themselves to keep it alive.

There is a traditional objection to every *imperium in imperio*, but this is only the jealousy of the tyrant. In actual fact, the modern State contains many organizations which it cannot defeat, except perhaps on rare occasions when public opinion is roused against them. Mr. Lloyd George's long fight with the medical profession over the Insurance Act was full of Homeric fluctuations of fortune. The Welsh miners recently routed the whole power of the State, backed by an excited nation. As for the financiers, no Government would dream of a conflict with them. When all other classes are exhorted to patriotism, they are allowed their 4½ per cent. and an increase of interest on their consols. It is well understood on all sides that an appeal to *their* patriotism would show gross ignorance of the world. It is against the traditions of the State to extort their money by threatening to withdraw police protection. This is not due to the difficulty of such a measure, but only to the fact that great wealth wins genuine admiration from us all, and we cannot bear to think of a very rich man being treated with disrespect.

The existence of strong organizations within the State, such as trade unions, is not undesirable except from the point of view of the official who wishes to wield unlimited power, or of the rival organizations, such as federations of employers, which would prefer a disorganized adversary. In view of the vastness of the State, most men can find little political outlet for initiative except in subordinate organizations formed for specific purposes. Without an outlet for political initiative, men lose their social vigor and their interest in public affairs: they become a prey to corrupt wire-pullers, or to sensation-mongers who have the art of capturing a tired and vagrant attention. The cure for this is to increase rather than diminish the powers of voluntary organizations, to give every man a sphere of political activity small enough for his interest and his capacity, and to confine the functions of the State, as far as possible, to the maintenance of peace among rival interests. The essential merit of the State is that it prevents the internal use of force by private persons. Its essential demerits are, that it promotes the external use of force, and that, by its great size, it makes each individual feel impotent even in a democracy. I shall return in a later lecture to the question of preventing war. The prevention of the sense of individual impotence cannot be achieved by a return to the small City State, which would be as reactionary as a return to the days before machinery. It must be achieved by a method which is in the direction of present tendencies. Such a method would be the increasing devolution of positive political initiative to bodies formed voluntarily for specific purposes, leaving the State rather in the position of a federal authority or a court of arbitration. The State will then confine itself to insisting upon *some* settlement of rival interests: its only principle in deciding what is the right settlement will be an attempt to find the measure most acceptable, on the whole, to all the parties concerned. This is the direction in which democratic States naturally tend, except in so far as they are turned aside by war or the fear of war. So long as war remains a daily imminent danger, the State will remain a Moloch, sacrificing sometimes the life of the individual, and always his unfettered development, to the barren struggle for mastery in the competition with other States. In internal as in external affairs, the worst enemy of freedom is war.

# III

# WAR AS AN INSTITUTION

IN SPITE OF the fact that most nations at most times, are at peace, war is one of the permanent institutions of all free communities, just as Parliament is one of our permanent institutions in spite of the fact that it is not always sitting. It is war as a permanent institution that I wish to consider: why men tolerate it; why they ought not to tolerate it; what hope there is of their coming not to tolerate it; and how they could abolish it if they wished to do so.

War is a conflict between two groups, each of which attempts to kill and maim as many as possible of the other group in order to achieve some object which it desires. The object is generally either power or wealth. It is a pleasure to exercise authority over other men, and it is a pleasure to live on the produce of other men's labor. The victor in war can enjoy more of these delights than the vanquished. But war, like all other natural activities, is not so much prompted by the end which it has in view as by an impulse to the activity itself. Very often men desire an end, not on its own account, but because their nature demands the actions which will lead to the end. And so it is in this case: the ends to be achieved by war appear in prospect far more important than they will appear when they are realized, because war itself is a fulfilment of one side of our nature. If men's actions sprang from desires for what would in fact bring happiness, the purely rational arguments against war would have long ago put an end to it. What makes war difficult to suppress is that it springs from an impulse, rather than from a calculation of the advantages to be derived from war.

War differs from the employment of force by the police through the fact that the actions of the police are ordered by a neutral authority, whereas in war it is the parties to the dispute themselves who set force in motion. This distinction is not absolute, since the State is not always wholly neutral in internal disturbances. When strikers are shot down, the State is taking the side of the rich. When opinions adverse to the existing State are punished, the State is obviously one of the parties to the dispute. And from the suppression of individual opinion up to civil war all gradations are possible. But broadly speaking, force employed according to laws previously laid down by the community as a whole may be distinguished from force employed by one community against another on occasions of which the one community is the sole judge. I have dwelt upon this difference because I do not think the use of force by the police can be wholly eliminated, and I think a similar use of force in international affairs is the best hope of permanent peace. At present, international affairs are regulated by the principle that a nation must not intervene unless its interests are involved: diplomatic usage forbids intervention for the mere maintenance of international law. America may protest when American citizens are drowned by German submarines, but must not protest when no American citizens are involved. The case would be analogous in internal affairs if the police would only interfere with murder when it happened that a policeman had been killed. So long as this principle prevails in the relations of States, the power of neutrals cannot be effectively employed to prevent war.

In every civilized country two forces coöperate to produce war. In ordinary times some men—usually a small proportion of the population—are bellicose: they predict war, and obviously are not unhappy in the prospect. So long as war is not imminent, the bulk of the population pay little attention to these men, and do not actively either support or oppose them. But when war begins to seem very near, a war fever seizes hold of people, and those who were already bellicose find themselves enthusiastically supported by all but an insignificant minority. The impulses which inspire war fever are rather different from those which make some men bellicose in ordinary times. Only educated men are likely to be warlike at ordinary times, since they alone are vividly aware of other countries or of the part which their own nation might play in the affairs of the world. But it is only their knowledge, not their nature, that distinguishes them from their more ignorant compatriots.

To take the most obvious example, German policy, in recent years before the war, was not averse from war, and not friendly to England. It is worth while to try to understand the state of mind from which this policy sprang.

The men who direct German policy are, to begin with, patriotic to an extent which is almost unknown in France and England. The interests of Germany appear to them unquestionably the only interests they need take into account. What injury may, in pursuing those interests, be done to other nations, what destruction may be brought upon populations and cities, what irreparable damage may result to civilization, it is not for them to consider. If they can confer what they regard as benefits upon Germany, everything else is of no account.

The second noteworthy point about German policy is that its conception of national welfare is mainly competitive. It is not the *intrinsic* wealth of Germany, whether materially or mentally, that the rulers of Germany consider important: it is the *comparative* wealth in the competition with other civilized countries. For this reason the destruction of good things abroad appears to them almost as desirable as the creation of good things in Germany. In most parts of the world the French are regarded as the most civilized of nations: their art and their literature and their way of life have an attraction for foreigners which those of Germany do not have. The English have developed political liberty, and the art of maintaining an Empire with a minimum of coercion, in a way for which Germany, hitherto, has shown no aptitude. These are grounds for envy, and envy wishes to destroy what is good in other countries. German militarists, quite rightly, judged that what was best in France and England would probably be destroyed by a great war, even if France and England were not in the end defeated in the actual fighting. I have seen a list of young French writers killed on the battlefield; probably the German authorities have also seen it, and have reflected with joy that another year of such losses will destroy French literature for a generation—perhaps, through loss of tradition, for ever. Every outburst against liberty in our more bellicose newspapers, every incitement to persecution of defenseless Germans, every mark of growing ferocity in our attitude, must be read with delight by German patriots, as proving their success in robbing us of our best, and in forcing us to imitate whatever is worst in Prussia.

But what the rulers of Germany have envied us most was power and wealth—the power derived from command of the seas and the straits, the wealth derived from a century of industrial supremacy. In both these respects they feel that their deserts are higher than ours. They have devoted far more thought and skill to military and industrial organization. Their average of intelligence and knowledge is far superior; their capacity for pursuing an attainable end, unitedly and with forethought, is infinitely greater. Yet we, merely (as they think) because we had a start in the race, have achieved a vastly larger Empire than they have, and an enormously greater control of capital. All this is unbearable; yet nothing but a great war can alter it.

Besides all these feelings, there is in many Germans, especially in those who know us best, a hot hatred of us on account of our pride. Farinata degli Uberti surveyed Hell "*come avesse lo Inferno in gran dispitto.*" Just so, by German accounts, English officer prisoners look round them among their captors—holding aloof, as though the enemy were noxious, unclean creatures, toads or slugs or centipedes, which a man does not touch willingly, and shakes off with loathing if he is forced to touch them for a moment. It is easy to imagine how the devils hated Farinata, and inflicted greater pains upon him than upon his neighbors, hoping to win recognition by some slight wincing on his part, driven to frenzy by his continuing to behave as if they did not exist. In just the same way the Germans are maddened by our spiritual immobility. At bottom we have regarded the Germans as one regards flies on a hot day: they are a nuisance, one has to brush them off, but it would not occur to one to be turned aside by them. Now that the initial certainty of victory has faded, we begin to be affected inwardly by the Germans. In time, if we continue to fail in our military enterprises, we shall realize that they are human beings, not just a tiresome circumstance. Then perhaps we shall hate them with a hatred which they will have no reason to resent. And from such a hatred it will be only a short journey to a genuine *rapprochement.*

The problem which must be solved, if the future of the world is to be less terrible than its present, is the problem of preventing nations from getting into the moods of England and Germany at the outbreak of the war. These two nations as they were at that moment might be taken as almost mythical representatives of pride and envy—cold pride and hot envy. Germany declaimed passionately: "You, England, swollen and decrepit, you overshadow my whole growth—your rotting branches keep the sun from shining upon me and the rain from nourishing me. Your spreading foliage must be lopped, your symmetrical beauty must be destroyed, that I too may have freedom to grow, that my young vigor may no longer be impeded by your decaying mass." England, bored and aloof, unconscious of the claims of outside forces, attempted absent-mindedly to sweep away the upstart disturber of meditation; but the upstart was not swept away, and remains so far with every prospect of making good his claim. The claim and the resistance to it are alike folly. Germany had no good ground for envy; we had no good ground for resisting whatever in Germany's demands was compatible with our continued existence. Is there any method of averting such reciprocal folly in the future?

I think if either the English or the Germans were capable of thinking in terms of individual welfare rather than national pride, they would have seen that, at every moment during the war the wisest course would have been to conclude peace at once, on the best terms that could have been obtained. This course, I am convinced, would have been the wisest for each separate nation, as well as for civilization in general. The utmost evil that the enemy could inflict through an unfavorable peace would be a trifle compared to the evil which all the nations inflict upon themselves by continuing to fight. What blinds us to this obvious fact is pride, the pride which makes the acknowledgment of defeat intolerable, and clothes itself in the garb of reason by suggesting all kinds of evils which are supposed to result from admitting defeat. But the only real evil of defeat is humiliation, and humiliation is subjective; we shall not feel humiliated if we become persuaded that it was a mistake to engage in the war, and that it is better to pursue other tasks not dependent upon world-dominion. If either the English or the Germans could admit this inwardly, any peace which did not destroy national independence could be accepted without real loss in the self-respect which is essential to a good life.

The mood in which Germany embarked upon the war was abominable, but it was a mood fostered by the habitual mood of England. We have prided ourselves upon our territory and our wealth; we have been ready at all times to defend by force of arms what we have conquered in India and Africa. If we had realized the futility of empire, and had shown a willingness to yield colonies to Germany without waiting for the threat of force, we might have been in a position to persuade the Germans that their ambitions were foolish, and that the respect of the world was not to be won by an imperialist policy. But by our resistance we showed that we shared their standards. We, being in possession, became enamored of the *status quo*. The Germans were willing to make war to upset the *status quo*; we were willing to make war to prevent its being upset in Germany's favor. So convinced were we of the sacredness of the *status quo* that we never realized how advantageous it was to us, or how, by insisting upon it, we shared the responsibility for the war. In a world where nations grow and decay, where forces change and populations become cramped, it is not possible or desirable to maintain the *status quo* for ever. If peace is to be preserved, nations must learn to accept unfavorable alterations of the map without feeling that they must first be defeated in war, or that in yielding they incur a humiliation.

It is the insistence of legalists and friends of peace upon the maintenance of the *status quo* that has driven Germany into militarism.

Germany had as good a right to an Empire as any other Great Power, but could only acquire an Empire through war. Love of peace has been too much associated with a static conception of international relations. In economic disputes we all know that whatever is vigorous in the wage-earning classes is opposed to "industrial peace," because the existing distribution of wealth is felt to be unfair. Those who enjoy a privileged position endeavor to bolster up their claims by appealing to the desire for peace, and decrying those who promote strife between the classes. It never occurs to them that by opposing changes without considering whether they are just, the capitalists share the responsibility for the class war. And in exactly the same way England shares the responsibility for Germany's war. If actual war is ever to cease there will have to be political methods of achieving the results which now can only be achieved by successful fighting, and nations will have voluntarily to admit adverse claims which appear just in the judgment of neutrals.

It is only by some such admission, embodying itself in a Parliament of the nations with full power to alter the distribution of territory, that militarism can be permanently overcome. It may be that the present war will bring, in the Western nations, a change of mood and outlook sufficient to make such an institution possible. It may be that more wars and more destruction will be necessary before the majority of civilized men rebel against the brutality and futile destruction of modern war. But unless our standards of civilization and our powers of constructive thought are to be permanently lowered, I cannot doubt that, sooner or later, reason will conquer the blind impulses which now lead nations into war. And if a large majority of the Great Powers had a firm determination that peace should be preserved, there would be no difficulty in devising diplomatic machinery for the settlement of disputes, and in establishing educational systems which would implant in the minds of the young an ineradicable horror of the slaughter which they are now taught to admire.

Besides the conscious and deliberate forces leading to war, there are the inarticulate feelings of common men, which, in most civilized countries, are always ready to burst into war fever at the bidding of statesmen. If peace is to be secure, the readiness to catch war fever must be somehow diminished. Whoever wishes to succeed in this must first understand what war fever is and why it arises.

The men who have an important influence in the world, whether for good or evil, are dominated as a rule by a threefold desire: they desire, first, an activity which calls fully into play the faculties in which they feel that they excel; secondly, the sense of successfully overcoming resistance; thirdly, the respect of others on account of their success. The third of these desires is sometimes absent: some men who have been great have been without the "last infirmity," and have been content with their own sense of success, or merely with the joy of difficult effort. But as a rule all three are present. Some men's talents are specialized, so that their choice of activities is circumscribed by the nature of their faculties; other men have, in youth, such a wide range of possible aptitudes that their choice is chiefly determined by the varying degrees of respect which public opinion gives to different kinds of success.

The same desires, usually in a less marked degree, exist in men who have no exceptional talents. But such men cannot achieve anything very difficult by their individual efforts; for them, as units, it is impossible to acquire the sense of greatness or the triumph of strong resistance overcome. Their separate lives are unadventurous and dull. In the morning they go to the office or the plow, in the evening they return tired and silent, to the sober monotony of wife and children. Believing that security is the supreme good, they have insured against sickness and death, and have found an employment where they have little fear of dismissal and no hope of any great rise. But security, once achieved, brings a Nemesis of ennui. Adventure, imagination, risk, also have their claims; but how can these claims be satisfied by the ordinary wage-earner? Even if it were possible to satisfy them, the claims of wife and children have priority and must not be neglected.

To this victim of order and good organization the realization comes, in some moment of sudden crisis, that he belongs to a nation, that his nation may take risks, may engage in difficult enterprises, enjoy the hot passion of doubtful combat, stimulate adventure and imagination by military expeditions to Mount Sinai and the Garden of Eden. What his nation does, in some sense, he does; what his nation suffers, he suffers. The long years of private caution are avenged by a wild plunge into public madness. All the horrid duties of thrift and order and care which he has learnt to fulfil in private are thought not to apply to public affairs: it is patriotic and noble to be reckless for the nation, though it would be wicked to be reckless for oneself. The old primitive passions, which civilization has denied, surge up all the stronger for repression. In a moment imagination and instinct travel back through the centuries, and the wild man of the woods emerges from the mental prison in which he has been confined. This is the deeper part of the psychology of the war fever.

But besides the irrational and instinctive element in the war fever, there is always also, if only as a liberator of primitive impulse, a certain amount of quasi-rational calculation and what is euphemistically called "thought." The war fever very seldom seizes a nation unless it believes that it will be victorious. Undoubtedly, under the influence of excitement, men over-estimate their chances of success; but there is some proportion between what is hoped and what a rational man would expect. Holland, though quite as humane as England, had no impulse to go to war on behalf of Belgium, because the likelihood of disaster was so obviously overwhelming. The London populace, if they had known how the war was going to develop, would not have rejoiced as they did on that August Bank Holiday long ago. A nation which has had a recent experience of war, and has come to know that a war is almost always more painful than it is expected to be at the outset, becomes much less liable to war fever until a new generation grows up. The element of rationality in war fever is recognized by Governments and journalists who desire war, as may be seen by their invariably minimizing the perils of a war which they wish to provoke. At the beginning of the South African War Sir William Butler was dismissed, apparently for suggesting that sixty thousand men and three months might not suffice to subdue the Boer Republics. And when the war proved long and difficult, the nation turned against those who had made it. We may assume, I think, without attributing too great a share to reason in human affairs, that a nation would not suffer from war fever in a case where every sane man could see that defeat was very probable.

The importance of this lies in the fact that it would make aggressive war very unlikely if its chances of success were very small. If the peace-loving nations were sufficiently strong to be obviously capable of defeating the nations which were willing to wage aggressive war, the peace-loving nations might form an alliance and agree to fight jointly against any nation which refused to submit its claims to an International Council. Before the present war we might have reasonably hoped to secure the peace of the world in some such way; but the military strength of Germany has shown that such a scheme has no great chance of success at present. Perhaps at some not far distant date it may be made more feasible by developments of policy in America.

The economic and political forces which make for war could be easily curbed if the will to peace existed strongly in all civilized nations. But so long as the populations are liable to war fever, all work for peace must be precarious; and if war fever could not be aroused, political and economic forces would be powerless to produce any long or very destructive war. The fundamental problem for the pacifist is to prevent the impulse towards war which seizes whole communities from time to time. And this can only be done by far-reaching changes in education, in the economic structure of society, and in the moral code by which public opinion controls the lives of men and women.[1]

A great many of the impulses which now lead nations to go to war are in themselves essential to any vigorous or progressive life. Without imagination and love of adventure a society soon becomes stagnant and begins to decay. Conflict, provided it is not destructive and brutal, is necessary in order to stimulate men's activities, and to secure the victory of what is living over what is dead or merely traditional. The wish for the triumph of one's cause, the sense of solidarity with large bodies of men, are not things which a wise man will wish to destroy. It is only the outcome in death and destruction and hatred that is evil. The problem is, to keep these impulses, without making war the outlet for them.

All Utopias that have hitherto been constructed are intolerably dull. Any man with any force in him would rather live in this world, with all its ghastly horrors, than in Plato's Republic or among Swift's Houyhnhnms. The men who make Utopias proceed upon a radically false assumption as to what constitutes a good life. They conceive that it is possible to imagine a certain state of society and a certain way of life which should be once for all recognized as good, and should then continue for ever and ever. They do not realize that much the greater part of a man's happiness depends upon activity, and only a very small remnant consists in passive enjoyment. Even the pleasures which do consist in enjoyment are only satisfactory, to most men, when they come in the intervals of activity. Social reformers, like inventors of Utopias, are apt to forget this very obvious fact of human nature. They aim rather at securing more leisure, and more opportunity for enjoying it, than at making work itself more satisfactory, more consonant with impulse, and a better outlet for creativeness and the desire to employ one's faculties. Work, in the modern world, is, to almost all who depend on earnings, mere work, not an embodiment of the desire for activity. Probably this is to a considerable extent inevitable. But in so far as it can be prevented something will be done to give a peaceful outlet to some of the impulses which lead to war.

---

1    These changes, which are to be desired on their own account, not only in order to prevent war, will be discussed in later lectures.

It would, of course, be easy to bring about peace if there were no vigor in the world. The Roman Empire was pacific and unproductive; the Athens of Pericles was the most productive and almost the most warlike community known to history. The only form of production in which our own age excels is science, and in science Germany, the most warlike of Great Powers, is supreme. It is useless to multiply examples; but it is plain that the very same vital energy which produces all that is best also produces war and the love of war. This is the basis of the opposition to pacifism felt by many men whose aims and activities are by no means brutal. Pacifism, in practice, too often expresses merely lack of force, not the refusal to use force in thwarting others. Pacifism, if it is to be both victorious and beneficent, must find an outlet, compatible with humane feeling, for the vigor which now leads nations into war and destruction.

This problem was considered by William James in an admirable address on "The Moral Equivalent of War," delivered to a congress of pacifists during the Spanish-American War of 1898. His statement of the problem could not be bettered; and so far as I know, he is the only writer who has faced the problem adequately. But his solution is not adequate; perhaps no adequate solution is possible. The problem, however, is one of degree: every additional peaceful outlet for men's energies diminishes the force which urges nations towards war, and makes war less frequent and less fierce. And as a question of degree, it is capable of more or less partial solutions.[2]

Every vigorous man needs some kind of contest, some sense of resistance overcome, in order to feel that he is exercising his faculties. Under the influence of economics, a theory has grown up that what men desire is wealth; this theory has tended to verify itself, because people's actions are more often determined by what they think they desire than by what they really desire. The less active members of a community often do in fact desire wealth, since it enables them to gratify a taste for passive enjoyment, and to secure respect without exertion. But the energetic men who make great fortunes seldom desire the actual money: they desire the sense of power through a contest, and the joy of successful activity. For this reason, those who are the most ruthless in making money are often the most willing to give it away; there are many notorious examples of this among American millionaires. The only element of truth in the economic theory that these men

---

2    What is said on this subject in the present lecture is only preliminary, since the subsequent lectures all deal with some aspect of the same problem.

are actuated by desire for money is this: owing to the fact that money is what is *believed* to be desirable, the making of money is recognized as the test of success. What is desired is visible and indubitable success; but this can only be achieved by being one of the few who reach a goal which many men would wish to reach. For this reason, public opinion has a great influence in directing the activities of vigorous men. In America a millionaire is more respected than a great artist; this leads men who might become either the one or the other to choose to become millionaires. In Renaissance Italy great artists were more respected than millionaires, and the result was the opposite of what it is in America.

Some pacifists and all militarists deprecate social and political conflicts. In this the militarists are in the right, from their point of view; but the pacifists seem to me mistaken. Conflicts of party politics, conflicts between capital and labor, and generally all those conflicts of principle which do not involve war, serve many useful purposes, and do very little harm. They increase men's interest in public affairs, they afford a comparatively innocent outlet for the love of contest, and they help to alter laws and institutions, when changing conditions or greater knowledge create the wish for an alteration. Everything that intensifies political life tends to bring about a peaceful interest of the same kind as the interest which leads to desire for war. And in a democratic community political questions give every voter a sense of initiative and power and responsibility which relieves his life of something of its narrow unadventurousness. The object of the pacifist should be to give men more and more political control over their own lives, and in particular to introduce democracy into the management of industry, as the syndicalists advise.

The problem for the reflective pacifist is two-fold: how to keep his own country at peace, and how to preserve the peace of the world. It is impossible that the peace of the world should be preserved while nations are liable to the mood in which Germany entered upon the war—unless, indeed, one nation were so obviously stronger than all others combined as to make war unnecessary for that one and hopeless for all the others. As this war has dragged on its weary length, many people must have asked themselves whether national independence is worth the price that has to be paid for it. Would it not perhaps be better to secure universal peace by the supremacy of one Power? "To secure peace by a world federation"—so a submissive pacifist may argue—"would require some faint glimmerings of reason in rulers and peoples, and is therefore out of the question; but to secure it by allowing Germany to dictate terms to Europe would be easy, in view of Germany's amazing military success. Since there is no other way of ending war"—so our advocate of peace at any price would contend—"let us adopt this way, which happens at the moment to be open to us." It is worth while to consider this view more attentively than is commonly considered.

There is one great historic example of a long peace secured in this way; I mean the Roman Empire. We in England boast of the *Pax Britannica* which we have imposed, in this way, upon the warring races and religions in India. If we are right in boasting of this, if we have in fact conferred a benefit upon India by enforced peace, the Germans would be right in boasting if they could impose a *Pax Germanica* upon Europe. Before the war, men might have said that India and Europe are not analogous, because India is less civilized than Europe; but now, I hope, no one would have the effrontery to maintain anything so preposterous. Repeatedly in modern history there has been a chance of achieving European unity by the hegemony of a single State; but always England, in obedience to the doctrine of the Balance of Power, has prevented this consummation, and preserved what our statesmen have called the "liberties of Europe." It is this task upon which we are now engaged. But I do not think our statesmen, or any others among us, have made much effort to consider whether the task is worth what it costs.

In one case we were clearly wrong: in our resistance to revolutionary France. If revolutionary France could have conquered the Continent and Great Britain, the world would now be happier, more civilized, and more free, as well as more peaceful. But revolutionary France was a quite exceptional case, because its early conquests were made in the name of liberty, against tyrants, not against peoples; and everywhere the French armies were welcomed as liberators by all except rulers and bigots. In the case of Philip II we were as clearly right as we were wrong in 1793. But in both cases our action is not to be judged by some abstract diplomatic conception of the "liberties of Europe," but by the ideals of the Power seeking hegemony, and by the probable effect upon the welfare of ordinary men and women throughout Europe.

"Hegemony" is a very vague word, and everything turns upon the degree of interference with liberty which it involves. There is a degree of interference with liberty which is fatal to many forms of national life; for example, Italy in the seventeenth and eighteenth centuries was crushed by the supremacy of Spain and Austria. If the Germans were actually to annex French provinces, as they did in 1871, they would probably inflict a serious injury upon those provinces, and make them less fruitful for civilization in general. For such reasons national liberty is a matter of real importance, and a Europe actually governed by Germany would probably be very dead and unproductive. But if "hegemony" merely means increased weight in diplomatic questions, more coaling stations and possessions in Africa, more power of securing advantageous commercial treaties, then it can hardly be supposed that it would do any vital damage to other nations; certainly it would not do so much damage as the present war is doing. I cannot doubt that, before the war, a hegemony of this kind would have abundantly satisfied the Germans. But the effect of the war, so far, has been to increase immeasurably all the dangers which it was intended to avert. We have now only the choice between certain exhaustion of Europe in fighting Germany and possible damage to the national life of France by German tyranny. Stated in terms of civilization and human welfare, not in terms of national prestige, that is now in fact the issue.

Assuming that war is not ended by one State conquering all the others, the only way in which it can be permanently ended is by a world-federation. So long as there are many sovereign States, each with its own Army, there can be no security that there will not be war. There will have to be in the world only one Army and one Navy before there will be any reason to think that wars have ceased. This means that, so far as the military functions of the State are concerned, there will be only one State, which will be world-wide.

The civil functions of the State—legislative, administrative, and judicial—have no very essential connection with the military functions, and there is no reason why both kinds of functions should normally be exercised by the same State. There is, in fact, every reason why the civil State and the military State should be different. The greater modern States are already too large for most civil purposes, but for military purposes they are not large enough, since they are not world-wide. This difference as to the desirable area for the two kinds of State introduces a certain perplexity and hesitation, when it is not realized that the two functions have little necessary connection: one set of considerations points towards small States, the other towards continually larger States. Of course, if there were an international Army and Navy, there would have to be some international authority to set them in motion. But this authority need never concern itself with any of the internal affairs of national States: it need only declare the rules which should regulate their relations, and pronounce judicially when those rules have been so infringed as to call for the intervention of the international force. How easily the limit of the authority could be fixed may be seen by many actual examples.

The civil and military State are often different in practice, for many purposes. The South American Republics are sovereign for all purposes except their relations with Europe, in regard to which they are subject to the United States: in dealings with Europe, the Army and Navy of the United States are their Army and Navy. Our self-governing Dominions depend for their defense, not upon their own forces but upon our Navy. Most Governments, nowadays, do not aim at formal annexation of a country which they wish to incorporate, but only at a protectorate—that is, civil autonomy subject to military control. Such autonomy is, of course, in practice incomplete, because it does not enable the "protected" country to adopt measures which are vetoed by the Power in military control. But it may be very nearly complete, as in the case of our self-governing Dominions. At the other extreme, it may become a mere farce, as in Egypt. In the case of an alliance, there is complete autonomy of the separate allied countries, together with what is practically a combination of their military forces into one single force.

The great advantage of a large military State is that it increases the area over which internal war is not possible except by revolution. If England and Canada have a disagreement, it is taken as a matter of course that a settlement shall be arrived at by discussion, not by force. Still more is this the case if Manchester and Liverpool have a quarrel, in spite of the fact that each is autonomous for many local purposes. No one would have thought it reasonable that Liverpool should go to war to prevent the construction of the Manchester Ship Canal, although almost any two Great Powers would have gone to war over an issue of the same relative importance. England and Russia would probably have gone to war over Persia if they had not been allies; as it is, they arrived by diplomacy at much the same iniquitous result as they would otherwise have reached by fighting. Australia and Japan would probably fight if they were both completely independent; but both depend for their liberties upon the British Navy, and therefore they have to adjust their differences peaceably.

The chief disadvantage of a large military State is that, when external war occurs, the area affected is greater. The quadruple Entente forms, for the present, one military State; the result is that, because of a dispute between Austria and Serbia, Belgium is devastated and Australians are killed in the Dardanelles. Another disadvantage is that it facilitates oppression. A large military State is practically omnipotent against a small State, and can impose its will, as England and Russia did in Persia and as Austria-Hungary has been doing in Serbia. It is impossible to make sure of avoiding oppression by any purely mechanical guarantees; only a liberal and humane spirit can afford a real protection. It has been perfectly possible for England to oppress Ireland, in spite of democracy and the presence of Irish Members at Westminster. Nor has the presence of Poles in the Reichstag prevented the oppression of Prussian Poland. But democracy and representative government undoubtedly make oppression less probable: they afford a means by which those who might be oppressed can cause their wishes and grievances to be publicly known, they render it certain that only a minority can be oppressed, and then only if the majority are nearly unanimous in wishing to oppress them. Also the practice of oppression affords much more pleasure to the governing classes, who actually carry it out, than to the mass of the population. For this reason the mass of the population, where it has power, is likely to be less tyrannical than an oligarchy or a bureaucracy.

In order to prevent war and at the same time preserve liberty it is necessary that there should be only one military State in the world, and that when disputes between different countries arise, it should act according to the decision of a central authority. This is what would naturally result from a federation of the world, if such a thing ever came about. But the prospect is remote, and it is worth while to consider why it is so remote.

The unity of a nation is produced by similar habits, instinctive liking, a common history, and a common pride. The unity of a nation is partly due to intrinsic affinities between its citizens, but partly also to the pressure and contrast of the outside world: if a nation were isolated, it would not have the same cohesion or the same fervor of patriotism. When we come to alliances of nations, it is seldom anything except outside pressure that produces solidarity. England and America, to some extent, are drawn together by the same causes which often make national unity: a (more or less) common language, similar political institutions, similar aims in international politics. But England, France, and Russia were drawn together solely by fear of Germany; if Germany had been annihilated by a natural cataclysm, they would at once have begun to hate one another, as they did before Germany was strong. For this reason, the possibility of coöperation in the present alliance against Germany affords no ground whatever for hoping that all the nations of the world might coöperate permanently in a peaceful alliance. The present motive for cohesion, namely a common fear, would be gone, and could not be replaced by any other motive unless men's thoughts and purposes were very different from what they are now.

The ultimate fact from which war results is not economic or political, and does not rest upon any mechanical difficulty of inventing means for the peaceful settlement of international disputes. The ultimate fact from which war results is the fact that a large proportion of mankind have an impulse to conflict rather than harmony, and can only be brought to coöperate with others in resisting or attacking a common enemy. This is the case in private life as well as in the relations of States. Most men, when they feel themselves sufficiently strong, set to work to make themselves feared rather than loved; the wish to gain the good opinion of others is confined, as a rule, to those who have not acquired secure power. The impulse to quarreling and self-assertion, the pleasure of getting one's own way in spite of opposition, is native to most men. It is this impulse, rather than any motive of calculated self-interest, which produces war, and causes the difficulty of bringing about a World-State. And this impulse is not confined to one nation; it exists, in varying degrees, in all the vigorous nations of the world.

But although this impulse is strong, there is no reason why it should be allowed to lead to war. It was exactly the same impulse which led to duelling; yet now civilized men conduct their private quarrels without bloodshed. If political contest within a World-State were substituted for war, imagination would soon accustom itself to the new situation, as it has accustomed itself to absence of duelling. Through the influence of institutions and habits, without any fundamental change in human nature, men would learn to look back upon war as we look upon the burning of heretics or upon human sacrifice to heathen deities. If I were to buy a revolver costing several pounds, in order to shoot my friend with a view to stealing sixpence out of his pocket, I should be thought neither very wise nor very virtuous. But if I can get sixty-five million accomplices to join me in this criminal absurdity, I become one of a great and glorious nation, nobly sacrificing the cost of my revolver, perhaps even my life, in order to secure the sixpence for the honor of my country. Historians, who are almost invariably sycophants, will praise me and my accomplices if we are successful, and say that we are worthy successors of the heroes who overthrew the might of Imperial Rome. But if my opponents are victorious, if their sixpences are defended at the cost of many pounds each and the lives of a large proportion of the population, then historians will call me a brigand (as I am), and praise the spirit and self-sacrifice of those who resisted me.

War is surrounded with glamour, by tradition, by Homer and the Old Testament, by early education, by elaborate myths as to the importance of the issues involved, by the heroism and self-sacrifice, which these myths call out. Jephthah sacrificing his daughter is a heroic figure, but he would have let her live if he had not been deceived by a myth. Mothers sending their sons to the battlefield are heroic, but they are as much deceived as Jephthah. And, in both cases alike, the heroism which issues in cruelty would be dispelled if there were not some strain of barbarism in the imaginative outlook from which myths spring. A God who can be pleased by the sacrifice of an innocent girl could only be worshiped by men to whom the thought of receiving such a sacrifice is not wholly abhorrent. A nation which believes that its welfare can only be secured by suffering and inflicting hundreds of thousands of equally horrible sacrifices, is a nation which has no very spiritual conception of what constitutes national welfare. It would be better a hundredfold to forgo material comfort, power, pomp, and outward glory than to kill and be killed, to hate and be hated, to throw away in a mad moment of fury the bright heritage of the ages. We have learnt gradually to free our God from the savagery with which the primitive Israelites and the Fathers endowed Him: few of us now believe that it is His pleasure to torture most of the human race in an eternity of hell-fire. But we have not yet learnt to free our national ideals from the ancient taint. Devotion to the nation is perhaps the deepest and most widespread religion of the present age. Like the ancient religions, it demands its persecutions, its holocausts, its lurid heroic cruelties; like them, it is noble, primitive, brutal, and mad. Now, as in the past, religion, lagging behind private consciences through the weight of tradition, steels the hearts of men against mercy and their minds against truth. If the world is to be saved, men must learn to be noble without being cruel, to be filled with faith and yet open to truth, to be inspired by great purposes without hating those who try to thwart them. But before this can happen, men must first face the terrible realization that the gods before whom they have bowed down were false gods and the sacrifices they have made were vain.

# IV

## PROPERTY

Among the many gloomy novelists of the realistic school, perhaps the most full of gloom is Gissing. In common with all his characters, he lives under the weight of a great oppression: the power of the fearful and yet adored idol of Money. One of his typical stories is "Eve's Ransom," where the heroine, with various discreditable subterfuges, throws over the poor man whom she loves in order to marry the rich man whose income she loves still better. The poor man, finding that the rich man's income has given her a fuller life and a better character than the poor man's love could have given her, decides that she has done quite right, and that he deserves to be punished for his lack of money. In this story, as in his other books, Gissing has set forth, quite accurately, the actual dominion of money, and the impersonal worship which it exacts from the great majority of civilized mankind.

Gissing's facts are undeniable, and yet his attitude produces a revolt in any reader who has vital passions and masterful desires. His worship of money is bound up with his consciousness of inward defeat. And in the modern world generally, it is the decay of life which has promoted the religion of material goods; and the religion of material goods, in its turn, has hastened the decay of life on which it thrives. The man who worships money has ceased to hope for happiness through his own efforts or in his own activities: he looks upon happiness as a passive enjoyment of pleasures derived from the outside world. The artist or the lover does not worship money in his moments of ardor, because his desires are specific, and directed towards objects which only he can create. And conversely, the worshiper of money can never achieve greatness as an artist or a lover.

Love of money has been denounced by moralists since the world began. I do not wish to add another to the moral denunciations, of which the efficacy in the past has not been encouraging. I wish to show how the worship of money is both an effect and a cause of diminishing vitality, and how our institutions might be changed so as to make the worship of money grow less and the general vitality grow more. It is not the desire for money as a means to definite ends that is in question. A struggling artist may desire money in order to have leisure for his art, but this desire is finite, and can be satisfied fully by a very modest sum. It is the *worship* of money that I wish to consider: the belief that all values may be measured in terms of money, and that money is the ultimate test of success in life. This belief is held in fact, if not in words, by multitudes of men and women, and yet it is not in harmony with human nature, since it ignores vital needs and the instinctive tendency towards some specific kind of growth. It makes men treat as unimportant those of their desires which run counter to the acquisition of money, and yet such desires are, as a rule, more important to well-being than any increase of income. It leads men to mutilate their own natures from a mistaken theory of what constitutes success, and to give admiration to enterprises which add nothing to human welfare. It promotes a dead uniformity of character and purpose, a diminution in the joy of life, and a stress and strain which leaves whole communities weary, discouraged, and disillusioned.

America, the pioneer of Western progress, is thought by many to display the worship of money in its most perfect form. A well-to-do American, who already has more than enough money to satisfy all reasonable requirements, almost always continues to work at his office with an assiduity which would only be pardonable if starvation were the alternative.

But England, except among a small minority, is almost as much given over to the worship of money as America. Love of money in England takes, as a rule, the form of snobbishly desiring to maintain a certain social status, rather than of striving after an indefinite increase of income. Men postpone marriage until they have an income enabling them to have as many rooms and servants in their house as they feel that their dignity requires. This makes it necessary for them while they are young to keep a watch upon their affections, lest they should be led into an imprudence: they acquire a cautious habit of mind, and a fear of "giving themselves away," which makes a free and vigorous life impossible. In acting as they do they imagine that they are being virtuous, since they would feel it a hardship for a woman to be asked to descend to a lower social status than that of her parents, and a degradation to themselves to marry a woman whose social status was not equal to their own. The things of nature are not valued in comparison with money. It is not thought a hardship for a woman to have to accept, as her only experience of love, the prudent and limited attentions of a man whose capacity for emotion has been lost during years of wise restraint or sordid relations with women whom he did not respect. The woman herself does not know that it is a hardship; for she, too, has been taught prudence for fear of a descent in the social scale, and from early youth she has had it instilled into her that strong feeling does not become a young woman. So the two unite to slip through life in ignorance of all that is worth knowing. Their ancestors were not restrained from passion by the fear of hell-fire, but they are restrained effectually by a worse fear, the fear of coming down in the world.

The same motives which lead men to marry late also lead them to limit their families. Professional men wish to send their sons to a public school, though the education they will obtain is no better than at a grammar school, and the companions with whom they will associate are more vicious. But snobdom has decided that public schools are best, and from its verdict there is no appeal. What makes them the best is that they are the most expensive. And the same social struggle, in varying forms, runs through all classes except the very highest and the very lowest. For this purpose men and women make great moral efforts, and show amazing powers of self-control; but all their efforts and all their self-control, being not used for any creative end, serve merely to dry up the well-spring of life within them, to make them feeble, listless, and trivial. It is not in such a soil that the passion which produces genius can be nourished. Men's souls have exchanged the wilderness for the drawing-room: they have become cramped and petty and deformed, like Chinese women's feet. Even the horrors of war have hardly awakened them from the smug somnambulism of respectability. And it is chiefly the worship of money that has brought about this deathlike slumber of all that makes men great.

In France the worship of money takes the form of thrift. It is not easy to make a fortune in France, but an inherited competence is very common, and where it exists the main purpose of life is to hand it on undiminished, if not increased. The French *rentier* is one of the great forces in international politics: it is he through whom France has been strengthened in diplomacy and weakened in war, by increasing the supply of French capital and diminishing the supply of French men. The necessity of providing a *dot* for daughters, and the subdivision of property by the law of inheritance, have made the family more powerful, as an institution, than in any other civilized country. In order that the family may prosper, it is kept small, and the individual members are often sacrificed to it. The desire for family continuity makes men timid and unadventurous: it is only in the organized proletariat that the daring spirit survives which made the Revolution and led the world in political thought and practice. Through the influence of money, the strength of the family has become a weakness to the nation by making the population remain stationary and even tend to decline. The same love of safety is beginning to produce the same effects elsewhere; but in this, as in many better things, France has led the way.

In Germany the worship of money is more recent than in France, England, and America; indeed, it hardly existed until after the Franco-Prussian War. But it has been adopted now with the same intensity and whole-heartedness which have always marked German beliefs. It is characteristic that, as in France the worship of money is associated with the family, so in Germany it is associated with the State. Liszt, in deliberate revolt against the English economists, taught his compatriots to think of economics in national terms, and the German who develops a business is felt, by others as well as by himself, to be performing a service to the State. Germans believe that England's greatness is due to industrialism and Empire, and that our success in these is due to an intense nationalism. The apparent internationalism of our Free Trade policy they regard as mere hypocrisy. They have set themselves to imitate what they believe we really are, with only the hypocrisy omitted. It must be admitted that their success has been amazing. But in the process they have destroyed almost all that made Germany of value to the world, and they have not adopted whatever of good there may have been among us, since that was all swept aside in the wholesale condemnation of "hypocrisy." And in adopting our worst faults, they have made them far worse by a system, a thoroughness, and a unanimity of which we are happily incapable. Germany's religion is of great importance to the world, since Germans have a power of real belief, and have the energy to acquire the virtues and vices which their creed demands. For the sake of the world, as well as for the sake of Germany, we must hope that they will soon abandon the worship of wealth which they have unfortunately learnt from us.

Worship of money is no new thing, but it is a more harmful thing than it used to be, for several reasons. Industrialism has made work more wearisome and intense, less capable of affording pleasure and interest by the way to the man who has undertaken it for the sake of money. The power of limiting families has opened a new field for the operation of thrift. The general increase in education and self-discipline has made men more capable of pursuing a purpose consistently in spite of temptations, and when the purpose is against life it becomes more destructive with every increase of tenacity in those who adopt it. The greater productivity resulting from industrialism has enabled us to devote more labor and capital to armies and navies for the protection of our wealth from envious neighbors, and for the exploitation of inferior races, which are ruthlessly wasted by the capitalist régime. Through the fear of losing money, forethought and anxiety eat away men's power of happiness, and the dread of misfortune becomes a greater misfortune than the one which is dreaded. The happiest men and women, as we can all testify from our own experience, are those who are indifferent to money because they have some positive purpose which shuts it out. And yet all our political thought, whether imperialist, radical, or socialist, continues to occupy itself almost exclusively with men's economic desires, as though they alone had real importance.

In judging of an industrial system, whether the one under which we live or one proposed by reformers, there are four main tests which may be applied. We may consider whether the system secures (1) the maximum of production, or (2) justice in distribution, or (3) a tolerable existence for producers, or (4) the greatest possible freedom and stimulus to vitality and progress. We may say, broadly, that the present system aims only at the first of these objects, while socialism aims at the second and third. Some defenders of the present system contend that technical progress is better promoted by private enterprise than it would be if industry were in the hands of the State; to this extent they recognize the fourth of the objects we have enumerated. But they recognize it only on the side of the goods and the capitalist, not on the side of the wage-earner. I believe that the fourth is much the most important of the objects to be aimed at, that the present system is fatal to it, and that orthodox socialism might well prove equally fatal.

One of the least questioned assumptions of the capitalist system is, that production ought to be increased in amount by every possible means: by new kinds of machinery, by employment of women and boys, by making hours of labor as long as is compatible with efficiency. Central African natives, accustomed to living on raw fruits of the earth and defeating Manchester by dispensing with clothes, are compelled to work by a hut tax which they can only pay by taking employment under European capitalists. It is admitted that they are perfectly happy while they remain free from European influences, and that industrialism brings upon them, not only the unwonted misery of confinement, but also death from diseases to which white men have become partially immune. It is admitted that the best negro workers are the "raw natives," fresh from the bush, uncontaminated by previous experience of wage-earning. Nevertheless, no one effectively contends that they ought to be preserved from the deterioration which we bring, since no one effectively doubts that it is good to increase the world's production at no matter what cost.

The belief in the importance of production has a fanatical irrationality and ruthlessness. So long as something is produced, what it is that is produced seems to be thought a matter of no account. Our whole economic system encourages this view, since fear of unemployment makes any kind of work a boon to wage-earners. The mania for increasing production has turned men's thoughts away from much more important problems, and has prevented the world from getting the benefits it might have got out of the increased productivity of labor.

When we are fed and clothed and housed, further material goods are needed only for ostentation.[1] With modern methods, a certain proportion of the population, without working long hours, could do all the work that is really necessary in the way of producing commodities. The time which is now spent in producing luxuries could be spent partly in enjoyment and country holidays, partly in better education, partly in work that is not manual or subserving manual work. We could, if we wished, have far more science and art, more diffused knowledge and mental cultivation, more leisure for wage-earners, and more capacity for intelligent pleasures. At present not only wages, but almost all earned incomes, can only be obtained by working much longer hours than men ought to work. A man who earns £800 a year by hard work could not, as a rule, earn £400 a year by half as much work. Often he could not earn anything if he were not willing to work practically all day and every day. Because of the excessive belief in the value of production, it is thought right and proper for men to work long hours, and the good that might result from shorter hours is not realized. And all the cruelties of the industrial system, not only in Europe but even more in the tropics, arouse only an occasional feeble protest from a few philanthropists. This is because, owing to the distortion produced by our present economic methods, men's conscious desires, in such matters, cover only a very small part, and that not the most important part, of the real needs affected by industrial work. If this is to be remedied, it can only be by a different

---

1    Except by that small minority who are capable of artistic enjoyment.

economic system, in which the relation of activity to needs will be less concealed and more direct.

The purpose of maximizing production will not be achieved in the long run if our present industrial system continues. Our present system is wasteful of human material, partly through damage to the health and efficiency of industrial workers, especially when women and children are employed, partly through the fact that the best workers tend to have small families and that the more civilized races are in danger of gradual extinction. Every great city is a center of race-deterioration. For the case of London this has been argued with a wealth of statistical detail by Sir H. Llewelyn Smith;[2] and it cannot easily be doubted that it is equally true in other cases. The same is true of material resources: the minerals, the virgin forests, and the newly developed wheatfields of the world are being exhausted with a reckless prodigality which entails almost a certainty of hardship for future generations.

Socialists see the remedy in State ownership of land and capital, combined with a more just system of distribution. It cannot be denied that our present system of distribution is indefensible from every point of view, including the point of view of justice. Our system of distribution is regulated by law, and is capable of being changed in many respects which familiarity makes us regard as natural and inevitable. We may distinguish four chief sources of recognized legal rights to private property: (1) a man's right to what he has made himself; (2) the right to interest on capital which has been lent; (3) the ownership of land; (4) inheritance. These form a crescendo of respectability: capital is more respectable than labor, land is more respectable than capital, and any form of wealth is more respectable when it is inherited than when it has been acquired by our own exertions.

A man's right to the produce of his own labor has never, in fact, had more than a very limited recognition from the law. The early socialists, especially the English forerunners of Marx, used to insist upon this right as the basis of a just system of distribution, but in the complication of modern industrial processes it is impossible to say what a man has produced. What proportion of the goods carried by a railway should belong to the goods porters concerned in their journey? When a surgeon saves a man's life by an operation, what proportion of the commodities which the man subsequently produces can the surgeon justly claim? Such problems are insoluble. And there is no special justice, even if they were soluble, in allowing to each man what

---

2   Booth's "Life and Labour of the People," vol. iii.

he himself produces. Some men are stronger, healthier, cleverer, than others, but there is no reason for increasing these natural injustices by the artificial injustices of the law. The principle recommends itself partly as a way of abolishing the very rich, partly as a way of stimulating people to work hard. But the first of these objects can be better obtained in other ways, and the second ceases to be obviously desirable as soon as we cease to worship money.

Interest arises naturally in any community in which private property is unrestricted and theft is punished, because some of the most economical processes of production are slow, and those who have the skill to perform them may not have the means of living while they are being completed. But the power of lending money gives such great wealth and influence to private capitalists that unless strictly controlled it is not compatible with any real freedom for the rest of the population. Its effects at present, both in the industrial world and in international politics, are so bad that it seems imperatively necessary to devise some means of curbing its power.

Private property in land has no justification except historically through power of the sword. In the beginning of feudal times, certain men had enough military strength to be able to force those whom they disliked not to live in a certain area. Those whom they chose to leave on the land became their serfs, and were forced to work for them in return for the gracious permission to stay. In order to establish law in place of private force, it was necessary, in the main, to leave undisturbed the rights which had been acquired by the sword. The land became the property of those who had conquered it, and the serfs were allowed to give rent instead of service. There is no justification for private property in land, except the historical necessity to conciliate turbulent robbers who would not otherwise have obeyed the law. This necessity arose in Europe many centuries ago, but in Africa the whole process is often quite recent. It is by this process, slightly disguised, that the Kimberley diamond mines and the Rand gold mines were acquired in spite of prior native rights. It is a singular example of human inertia that men should have continued until now to endure the tyranny and extortion which a small minority are able to inflict by their possession of the land. No good to the community, of any sort or kind, results from the private ownership of land. If men were reasonable, they would decree that it should cease to-morrow, with no compensation beyond a moderate life income to the present holders.

The mere abolition of rent would not remove injustice, since it would confer a capricious advantage upon the occupiers of the best sites and the most fertile land. It is necessary that there should be rent, but it should be paid to the State or to some body which performs public services; or, if the total rental were more than is required for such purposes, it might be paid into a common fund and divided equally among the population. Such a method would be just, and would not only help to relieve poverty, but would prevent wasteful employment of land and the tyranny of local magnates. Much that appears as the power of capital is really the power of the landowner—for example, the power of railway companies and mine-owners. The evil and injustice of the present system are glaring, but men's patience of preventable evils to which they are accustomed is so great that it is impossible to guess when they will put an end to this strange absurdity.

Inheritance, which is the source of the greater part of the unearned income in the world, is regarded by most men as a natural right. Sometimes, as in England, the right is inherent in the owner of property, who may dispose of it in any way that seems good to him. Sometimes, as in France, his right is limited by the right of his family to inherit at least a portion of what he has to leave. But neither the right to dispose of property by will nor the right of children to inherit from parents has any basis outside the instincts of possession and family pride.

There may be reasons for allowing a man whose work is exceptionally fruitful—for instance, an inventor—to enjoy a larger income than is enjoyed by the average citizen, but there can be no good reason for allowing this privilege to descend to his children and grandchildren and so on for ever. The effect is to produce an idle and exceptionally fortunate class, who are influential through their money, and opposed to reform for fear it should be directed against themselves. Their whole habit of thought becomes timid, since they dread being forced to acknowledge that their position is indefensible; yet snobbery and the wish to secure their favor leads almost the whole middle-class to ape their manners and adopt their opinions. In this way they become a poison infecting the outlook of almost all educated people.

It is sometimes said that without the incentive of inheritance men would not work so well. The great captains of industry, we are assured, are actuated by the desire to found a family, and would not devote their lives to unremitting toil without the hope of gratifying this desire. I do not believe that any large proportion of really useful work is done from this motive. Ordinary work is done for the sake of a living, and the very best work is done for the interest of the work itself. Even the captains of industry, who are thought (perhaps by themselves as well as by others) to be aiming at founding a family, are probably more actuated by love of power and by the adventurous pleasure of great enterprises. And if there were some slight diminution in the amount of work done, it would be well worth while in order to get rid of the idle rich, with the oppression, feebleness, and corruption which they inevitably introduce.

The present system of distribution is not based upon any principle. Starting from a system imposed by conquest, the arrangements made by the conquerors for their own benefit were stereotyped by the law, and have never been fundamentally reconstructed. On what principles ought the reconstruction to be based?

Socialism, which is the most widely advocated scheme of reconstruction, aims chiefly at *justice*: the present inequalities of wealth are unjust, and socialism would abolish them. It is not essential to socialism that all men should have the same income, but it is essential that inequalities should be justified, in each case, by inequality of need or of service performed. There can be no disputing that the present system is grossly unjust, and that almost all that is unjust in it is harmful. But I do not think justice alone is a sufficient principle upon which to base an economic reconstruction. Justice would be secured if all were equally unhappy, as well as if all were equally happy. Justice, by itself, when once realized, contains no source of new life. The old type of Marxian revolutionary socialist never dwelt, in imagination, upon the life of communities after the establishment of the millennium. He imagined that, like the Prince and Princess in a fairy story, they would live happily ever after. But that is not a condition possible to human nature. Desire, activity, purpose, are essential to a tolerable life, and a millennium, though it may be a joy in prospect, would be intolerable if it were actually achieved.

The more modern socialists, it is true, have lost most of the religious fervor which characterized the pioneers, and view socialism as a tendency rather than a definite goal. But they still retain the view that what is of most political importance to a man is his income, and that the principal aim of a democratic politician ought to be to increase the wages of labor. I believe this involves too passive a conception of what constitutes happiness. It is true that, in the industrial world, large sections of the population are too poor to have any possibility of a good life; but it is not true that a good life will come of itself with a diminution of poverty. Very few of the well-to-do classes have a good life at present, and perhaps socialism would only substitute the evils which now afflict the more prosperous in place of the evils resulting from destitution.

In the existing labor movement, although it is one of the most vital sources of change, there are certain tendencies against which reformers ought to be on their guard. The labor movement is in essence a movement in favor of justice, based upon the belief that the sacrifice of the many to the few is not necessary now, whatever may have been the case in the past. When labor was less productive and education was less widespread, an aristocratic civilization may have been the only one possible: it may have been necessary that the many should contribute to the life of the few, if the few were to transmit and increase the world's possessions in art and thought and civilized existence. But this necessity is past or rapidly passing, and there is no longer any valid objection to the claims of justice. The labor movement is morally irresistible, and is not now seriously opposed except by prejudice and simple self-assertion. All living thought is on its side; what is against it is traditional and dead. But although it itself is living, it is not by any means certain that it will make for life.

Labor is led by current political thought in certain directions which would become repressive and dangerous if they were to remain strong after labor had triumphed. The aspirations of the labor movement are, on the whole, opposed by the great majority of the educated classes, who feel a menace, not only or chiefly to their personal comfort, but to the civilized life in which they have their part, which they profoundly believe to be important to the world. Owing to the opposition of the educated classes, labor, when it is revolutionary and vigorous, tends to despise all that the educated classes represent. When it is more respectful, as its leaders tend to be in England, the subtle and almost unconscious influence of educated men is apt to sap revolutionary ardor, producing doubt and uncertainty instead of the swift, simple assurance by which victory might have been won. The very sympathy which the best men in the well-to-do classes extend to labor, their very readiness to admit the justice of its claims, may have the effect of softening the opposition of labor leaders to the *status quo*, and of opening their minds to the suggestion that no fundamental change is possible. Since these influences affect leaders much more than the rank and file, they tend to produce in the rank and file a distrust of leaders, and a desire to seek out new leaders who will be less ready to concede the claims of the more fortunate classes. The result may be in the end a labor movement as hostile to the life of the mind as some terrified property-owners believe it to be at present.

The claims of justice, narrowly interpreted, may reinforce this tendency. It may be thought unjust that some men should have larger incomes or shorter hours of work than other men. But efficiency in mental work, including the work of education, certainly requires more comfort and longer periods of rest than are required for efficiency in physical work, if only because mental work is not physiologically wholesome. If this is not recognized, the life of the mind may suffer through short-sightedness even more than through deliberate hostility.

Education suffers at present, and may long continue to suffer, through the desire of parents that their children should earn money as soon as possible. Every one knows that the half-time system, for example, is bad; but the power of organized labor keeps it in existence. It is clear that the cure for this evil, as for those that are concerned with the population question, is to relieve parents of the expense of their children's education, and at the same time to take away their right to appropriate their children's earnings.

The way to prevent any dangerous opposition of labor to the life of the mind is not to oppose the labor movement, which is too strong to be opposed with justice. The right way is, to show by actual practice that thought is useful to labor, that without thought its positive aims cannot be achieved, and that there are men in the world of thought who are willing to devote their energies to helping labor in its struggle. Such men, if they are wise and sincere, can prevent labor from becoming destructive of what is living in the intellectual world.

Another danger in the aims of organized labor is the danger of conservatism as to methods of production. Improvements of machinery or organization bring great advantages to employers, but involve temporary and sometimes permanent loss to the wage-earners. For this reason, and also from mere instinctive dislike of any change of habits, strong labor organizations are often obstacles to technical progress. The ultimate basis of all social progress must be increased technical efficiency, a greater result from a given amount of labor. If labor were to offer an effective opposition to this kind of progress, it would in the long run paralyze all other progress. The way to overcome the opposition of labor is not by hostility or moral homilies, but by giving to labor the direct interest in economical processes which now belongs to the employers. Here, as elsewhere, the unprogressive part of a movement which is essentially progressive is to be eliminated, not by decrying the whole movement but by giving it a wider sweep, making it more progressive, and leading it to demand an even greater change in the structure of society than any that it had contemplated in its inception.

The most important purpose that political institutions can achieve is to keep alive in individuals creativeness, vigor, vitality, and the joy of life. These things existed, for example, in Elizabethan England in a way in which they do not exist now. They stimulated adventure, poetry, music, fine architecture, and set going the whole movement out of which England's greatness has sprung in every direction in which England has been great. These things coexisted with injustice, but outweighed it, and made a national life more admirable than any that is likely to exist under socialism.

What is wanted in order to keep men full of vitality is opportunity, not security. Security is merely a refuge from fear; opportunity is the source of hope. The chief test of an economic system is not whether it makes men prosperous, or whether it secures distributive justice (though these are both very desirable), but whether it leaves men's instinctive growth unimpeded. To achieve this purpose, there are two main conditions which it should fulfil: it should not cramp men's private affections, and it should give the greatest possible outlet to the impulse of creation. There is in most men, until it becomes atrophied by disuse, an instinct of constructiveness, a wish to make something. The men who achieve most are, as a rule, those in whom this instinct is strongest: such men become artists, men of science, statesmen, empire-builders, or captains of industry, according to the accidents of temperament and opportunity. The most beneficent and the most harmful careers are inspired by this impulse. Without it, the world would sink to the level of Tibet: it would subsist, as it is always prone to do, on the wisdom of its ancestors, and each generation would sink more deeply into a lifeless traditionalism.

But it is not only the remarkable men who have the instinct of constructiveness, though it is they who have it most strongly. It is almost universal in boys, and in men it usually survives in a greater or less degree, according to the greater or less outlet which it is able to find. Work inspired by this instinct is satisfying, even when it is irksome and difficult, because every effort is as natural as the effort of a dog pursuing a hare. The chief defect of the present capitalistic system is that work done for wages very seldom affords any outlet for the creative impulse. The man who works for wages has no choice as to what he shall make: the whole creativeness of the processes concentrate in the employer who orders the work to be done. For this reason the work becomes a merely external means to a certain result, the earning of wages. Employers grow indignant about the trade union rules for limitation of output, but they have no right to be indignant, since they do not permit the men whom they employ to have any share in the purpose for which the work is undertaken. And so the process of production, which should form one instinctive cycle, becomes divided into separate purposes, which can no longer provide any satisfaction of instinct for those who do the work.

This result is due to our industrial system, but it would not be avoided by socialism. In a socialist community, the State would be the employer, and the individual workman would have almost as little control over his work as he has at present. Such control as he could exercise would be indirect, through political channels, and would be too slight and roundabout to afford any appreciable satisfaction. It is to be feared that instead of an increase of self-direction, there would only be an increase of mutual interference.

The total abolition of private capitalistic enterprise, which is demanded by Marxian socialism, seems scarcely necessary. Most men who construct sweeping systems of reform, like most of those who defend the *status quo*, do not allow enough for the importance of exceptions and the undesirability of rigid system. Provided the sphere of capitalism is restricted, and a large proportion of the population are rescued from its dominion, there is no reason to wish it wholly abolished. As a competitor and a rival, it might serve a useful purpose in preventing more democratic enterprises from sinking into sloth and technical conservatism. But it is of the very highest importance that capitalism should become the exception rather than the rule, and that the bulk of the world's industry should be conducted on a more democratic system.

Much of what is to be said against militarism in the State is also to be said against capitalism in the economic sphere. Economic organizations, in the pursuit of efficiency, grow larger and larger, and there is no possibility of reversing this process. The causes of their growth are technical, and large organizations must be accepted as an essential part of civilized society. But there is no reason why their government should be centralized and monarchical. The present economic system, by robbing most men of initiative, is one of the causes of the universal weariness which devitalizes urban and industrial populations, making them perpetually seek excitement, and leading them to welcome even the outbreak of war as a relief from the dreary monotony of their daily lives.

If the vigor of the nation is to be preserved, if we are to retain any capacity for new ideas, if we are not to sink into a Chinese condition of stereotyped immobility, the monarchical organization of industry must be swept away. All large businesses must become democratic and federal in their government. The whole wage-earning system is an abomination, not only because of the social injustice which it causes and perpetuates, but also because it separates the man who does the work from the purpose for which the work is done. The whole of the controlling purpose is concentrated in the capitalist; the purpose of the wage-earner is not the produce, but the wages. The purpose of the capitalist is to secure the maximum of work for the minimum of wages; the purpose of the wage-earner is to secure the maximum of wages for the minimum of work. A system involving this essential conflict of interests cannot be expected to work smoothly or successfully, or to produce a community with any pride in efficiency.

Two movements exist, one already well advanced, the other in its infancy, which seem capable, between them, of effecting most of what is needed. The two movements I mean are the coöperative movement and syndicalism. The coöperative movement is capable of replacing the wage system over a very wide field, but it is not easy to see how it could be applied to such things as railways. It is just in these cases that the principles of syndicalism are most easily applicable.

If organization is not to crush individuality, membership of an organization ought to be voluntary, not compulsory, and ought always to carry with it a voice in the management. This is not the case with economic organizations, which give no opportunity for the pride and pleasure that men find in an activity of their own choice, provided it is not utterly monotonous.

It must be admitted, however, that much of the mechanical work which is necessary in industry is probably not capable of being made interesting in itself. But it will seem less tedious than it does at present if those who do it have a voice in the management of their industry. And men who desire leisure for other occupations might be given the opportunity of doing uninteresting work during a few hours of the day for a low wage; this would give an opening to all who wished for some activity not immediately profitable to themselves. When everything that is possible has been done to make work interesting, the residue will have to be made endurable, as almost all work is at present, by the inducement of rewards outside the hours of labor. But if these rewards are to be satisfactory, it is essential that the uninteresting work should not necessarily absorb a man's whole energies, and that opportunities should exist for more or less continuous activities during the remaining hours. Such a system might be an immeasurable boon to artists, men of letters, and others who produce for their own satisfaction works which the public does not value soon enough to secure a living for the producers; and apart from such rather rare cases, it might provide an opportunity for young men and women with intellectual ambitions to continue their education after they have left school, or to prepare themselves for careers which require an exceptionally long training.

The evils of the present system result from the separation between the several interests of consumer, producer, and capitalist. No one of these three has the same interests as the community or as either of the other two. The coöperative system amalgamates the interests of consumer and capitalist; syndicalism would amalgamate the interests of producer and capitalist. Neither amalgamates all three, or makes the interests of those who direct industry quite identical with those of the community. Neither, therefore, would wholly prevent industrial strife, or obviate the need of the State as arbitrator. But either would be better than the present system, and probably a mixture of both would cure most of the evils of industrialism as it exists now. It is surprising that, while men and women have struggled to achieve political democracy, so little has been done to introduce democracy in industry. I believe incalculable benefits might result from industrial democracy, either on the coöperative model or with recognition of a trade or industry as a unit for purposes of government, with some kind of Home Rule such as syndicalism aims at securing. There is no reason why all governmental units should be geographical: this system was necessary in the past because of the slowness of means of communication, but it is not necessary now. By some such system many men might come to feel again a pride in their work, and to find again that outlet for the creative impulse which is now denied to all but a fortunate few. Such a system requires the abolition of the land-owner and the restriction of the capitalist, but does not entail equality of earnings. And unlike socialism, it is not a static or final system: it is hardly more than a framework for energy and initiative. It is only by some such method, I believe, that the free growth of the individual can be reconciled with the huge technical organizations which have been rendered necessary by industrialism.

# V

# EDUCATION

N O POLITICAL THEORY is adequate unless it is applicable to children
as well as to men and women. Theorists are mostly childless, or, if
they have children, they are carefully screened from the disturbances
which would be caused by youthful turmoil. Some of them have written books on education, but without, as a rule, having any actual children present to their minds while they wrote. Those educational theorists who have had a knowledge of children, such as the inventors of
Kindergarten and the Montessori system,[1] have not always had enough
realization of the ultimate goal of education to be able to deal successfully with advanced instruction. I have not the knowledge either of
children or of education which would enable me to supply whatever
defects there may be in the writings of others. But some questions,
concerning education as a political institution, are involved in any
hope of social reconstruction, and are not usually considered by writers on educational theory. It is these questions that I wish to discuss.

The power of education in forming character and opinion is very
great and very generally recognized. The genuine beliefs, though not
usually the professed precepts, of parents and teachers are almost
unconsciously acquired by most children; and even if they depart from
these beliefs in later life, something of them remains deeply implanted,
ready to emerge in a time of stress or crisis. Education is, as a rule,
the strongest force on the side of what exists and against fundamental
change: threatened institutions, while they are still powerful, possess
themselves of the educational machine, and instil a respect for their
own excellence into the malleable minds of the young. Reformers
retort by trying to oust their opponents from their position of vantage.
The children themselves are not considered by either party; they are
merely so much material, to be recruited into one army or the other.
If the children themselves were considered, education would not aim

---

1    As regards the education of young children, Madame Montessori's methods seem
to me full of wisdom.

at making them belong to this party or that, but at enabling them to choose intelligently between the parties; it would aim at making them able to think, not at making them think what their teachers think. Education as a political weapon could not exist if we respected the rights of children. If we respected the rights of children, we should educate them so as to give them the knowledge and the mental habits required for forming independent opinions; but education as a political institution endeavors to form habits and to circumscribe knowledge in such a way as to make one set of opinions inevitable.

The two principles of *justice* and *liberty*, which cover a very great deal of the social reconstruction required, are not by themselves sufficient where education is concerned. Justice, in the literal sense of equal rights, is obviously not wholly possible as regards children. And as for liberty, it is, to begin with, essentially negative: it condemns all avoidable interference with freedom, without giving a positive principle of construction. But education is essentially constructive, and requires some positive conception of what constitutes a good life. And although liberty is to be respected in education as much as is compatible with instruction, and although a very great deal more liberty than is customary can be allowed without loss to instruction, yet it is clear that some departure from complete liberty is unavoidable if children are to be taught anything, except in the case of unusually intelligent children who are kept isolated from more normal companions. This is one reason for the great responsibility which rests upon teachers: the children must, necessarily, be more or less at the mercy of their elders, and cannot make themselves the guardians of their own interests. Authority in education is to some extent unavoidable, and those who educate have to find a way of exercising authority in accordance with the *spirit* of liberty.

Where authority is unavoidable, what is needed is *reverence*. A man who is to educate really well, and is to make the young grow and develop into their full stature, must be filled through and through with the spirit of reverence. It is reverence towards others that is lacking in those who advocate machine-made cast-iron systems: militarism, capitalism, Fabian scientific organization, and all the other prisons into which reformers and reactionaries try to force the human spirit. In education, with its codes of rules emanating from a Government office, its large classes and fixed curriculum and overworked teachers, its determination to produce a dead level of glib mediocrity, the lack of reverence for the child is all but universal. Reverence requires imagination and vital warmth; it requires most imagination in respect of those who have least actual achievement or power. The child is weak and superficially foolish, the teacher is strong, and in an every-day sense wiser than the child. The teacher without reverence, or the bureaucrat without reverence, easily despises the child for these outward inferiorities. He thinks it is his duty to "mold" the child: in imagination he is the potter with the clay. And so he gives to the child some unnatural shape, which hardens with age, producing strains and spiritual dissatisfactions, out of which grow cruelty and envy, and the belief that others must be compelled to undergo the same distortions.

Tho man who has reverence will not think it his duty to "mold" the young. He feels in all that lives, but especially in human beings, and most of all in children, something sacred, indefinable, unlimited, something individual and strangely precious, the growing principle of life, an embodied fragment of the dumb striving of the world. In the presence of a child he feels an unaccountable humility—a humility not easily defensible on any rational ground, and yet somehow nearer to wisdom than the easy self-confidence of many parents and teachers. The outward helplessness of the child and the appeal of dependence make him conscious of the responsibility of a trust. His imagination shows him what the child may become, for good or evil, how its impulses may be developed or thwarted, how its hopes must be dimmed and the life in it grow less living, how its trust will be bruised and its quick desires replaced by brooding will. All this gives him a longing to help the child in its own battle; he would equip and strengthen it, not for some outside end proposed by the State or by any other impersonal authority, but for the ends which the child's own spirit is obscurely seeking. The man who feels this can wield the authority of an educator without infringing the principle of liberty.

It is not in a spirit of reverence that education is conducted by States and Churches and the great institutions that are subservient to them. What is considered in education is hardly ever the boy or girl, the young man or young woman, but almost always, in some form, the maintenance of the existing order. When the individual is considered, it is almost exclusively with a view to worldly success—making money or achieving a good position. To be ordinary, and to acquire the art of getting on, is the ideal which is set before the youthful mind, except by a few rare teachers who have enough energy of belief to break through the system within which they are expected to work. Almost all education has a political motive: it aims at strengthening some group, national or religious or even social, in the competition with other groups. It is this motive, in the main, which determines the subjects taught, the knowledge offered and the knowledge withheld, and also decides what mental habits the pupils are expected to acquire. Hardly anything is done to foster the inward growth of mind and spirit; in fact, those who have had most education are very often atrophied in their mental and spiritual life, devoid of impulse, and possessing only certain mechanical aptitudes which take the place of living thought.

Some of the things which education achieves at present must continue to be achieved by education in any civilized country. All children must continue to be taught how to read and write, and some must continue to acquire the knowledge needed for such professions as medicine or law or engineering. The higher education required for the sciences and the arts is necessary for those to whom it is suited. Except in history and religion and kindred matters, the actual instruction is only inadequate, not positively harmful. The instruction might be given in a more liberal spirit, with more attempt to show its ultimate uses; and of course much of it is traditional and dead. But in the main it is necessary, and would have to form a part of any educational system.

It is in history and religion and other controversial subjects that the actual instruction is positively harmful. These subjects touch the interests by which schools are maintained; and the interests maintain the schools in order that certain views on these subjects may be instilled. History, in every country, is so taught as to magnify that country: children learn to believe that their own country has always been in the right and almost always victorious, that it has produced almost all the great men, and that it is in all respects superior to all other countries. Since these beliefs are flattering, they are easily absorbed, and hardly ever dislodged from instinct by later knowledge.

To take a simple and almost trivial example: the facts about the battle of Waterloo are known in great detail and with minute accuracy; but the facts as taught in elementary schools will be widely different in England, France, and Germany. The ordinary English boy imagines that the Prussians played hardly any part; the ordinary German boy imagines that Wellington was practically defeated when the day was retrieved by Blücher's gallantry. If the facts were taught accurately in both countries, national pride would not be fostered to the same extent, neither nation would feel so certain of victory in the event of war, and the willingness to fight would be diminished. It is this result which has to be prevented. Every State wishes to promote national pride, and is conscious that this cannot be done by unbiased history. The defenseless children are taught by distortions and suppressions and suggestions. The false ideas as to the history of the world which are taught in the various countries are of a kind which encourages strife and serves to keep alive a bigoted nationalism. If good relations between States were desired, one of the first steps ought to be to submit all teaching of history to an international commission, which should produce neutral textbooks free from the patriotic bias which is now demanded everywhere.[2]

Exactly the same thing applies to religion. Elementary schools are practically always in the hands either of some religious body or of a State which has a certain attitude towards religion. A religious body exists through the fact that its members all have certain definite beliefs on subjects as to which the truth is not ascertainable. Schools conducted by religious bodies have to prevent the young, who are often inquiring by nature, from discovering that these definite beliefs are opposed by others which are no more unreasonable, and that many of the men best qualified to judge think that there is no good evidence in favor of any definite belief. When the State is militantly secular, as in France, State schools become as dogmatic as those that are in the hands of the Churches (I understand that the word "God" must not be mentioned in a French elementary school). The result in all these cases is the same: free inquiry is checked, and on the most important matter in the world the child is met with dogma or with stony silence.

It is not only in elementary education that these evils exist. In more advanced education they take subtler forms, and there is more attempt to conceal them, but they are still present. Eton and Oxford set a certain stamp upon a man's mind, just as a Jesuit College does. It can hardly be said that Eton and Oxford have a *conscious* purpose, but they have a purpose which is none the less strong and effective

---

2               The Teaching of Patriotism.
His Majesty's Approval.
The King has been graciously pleased to accept a copy of the little book containing suggestions to local education authorities and teachers in Wales as to the teaching of patriotism which has just been issued by the Welsh Department of the Board of Education in connection with the observance of the National Anniversary of St. David's Day. His Private Secretary (Lord Stamfordham), in writing to Mr. Alfred T. Davies, the Permanent Secretary of the Welsh Department, says that his Majesty is much pleased with the contents of the book, and trusts that the principles inculcated in it will bear good fruit in the lives and characters of the coming generation.—*Morning Post*, January 29, 1916.

for not being formulated. In almost all who have been through them they produce a worship of "good form," which is as destructive to life and thought as the medieval Church. "Good form" is quite compatible with a superficial open-mindedness, a readiness to hear all sides, and a certain urbanity towards opponents. But it is not compatible with fundamental open-mindedness, or with any inward readiness to give weight to the other side. Its essence is the assumption that what is most important is a certain kind of behavior, a behavior which minimizes friction between equals and delicately impresses inferiors with a conviction of their own crudity. As a political weapon for preserving the privileges of the rich in a snobbish democracy it is unsurpassable. As a means of producing an agreeable social *milieu* for those who have money with no strong beliefs or unusual desires it has some merit. In every other respect it is abominable.

The evils of "good form" arise from two sources: its perfect assurance of its own rightness, and its belief that correct manners are more to be desired than intellect, or artistic creation, or vital energy, or any of the other sources of progress in the world. Perfect assurance, by itself, is enough to destroy all mental progress in those who have it. And when it is combined with contempt for the angularities and awkwardnesses that are almost invariably associated with great mental power, it becomes a source of destruction to all who come in contact with it. "Good form" is itself dead and incapable of growth; and by its attitude to those who are without it it spreads its own death to many who might otherwise have life. The harm which it has done to well-to-do Englishmen, and to men whose abilities have led the well-to-do to notice them, is incalculable.

The prevention of free inquiry is unavoidable so long as the purpose of education is to produce belief rather than thought, to compel the young to hold positive opinions on doubtful matters rather than to let them see the doubtfulness and be encouraged to independence of mind. Education ought to foster the wish for truth, not the conviction that some particular creed is the truth. But it is creeds that hold men together in fighting organizations: Churches, States, political parties. It is intensity of belief in a creed that produces efficiency in fighting: victory comes to those who feel the strongest certainty about matters on which doubt is the only rational attitude. To produce this intensity of belief and this efficiency in fighting, the child's nature is warped, and its free outlook is cramped, by cultivating inhibitions as a check to the growth of new ideas. In those whose minds are not very active the result is the omnipotence of prejudice; while the few whose thought cannot be wholly killed become cynical, intellectually hopeless, destructively critical, able to make all that is living seem foolish, unable themselves to supply the creative impulses which they destroy in others.

The success in fighting which is achieved by suppressing freedom of thought is brief and very worthless. In the long run mental vigor is as essential to success as it is to a good life. The conception of education as a form of drill, a means of producing unanimity through slavishness, is very common, and is defended chiefly on the ground that it leads to victory. Those who enjoy parallels from ancient history will point to the victory of Sparta over Athens to enforce their moral. But it is Athens that has had power over men's thoughts and imaginations, not Sparta: any one of us, if we could be born again into some past epoch, would rather be born an Athenian than a Spartan. And in the modern world so much intellect is required in practical affairs that even the external victory is more likely to be won by intelligence than by docility. Education in credulity leads by quick stages to mental decay; it is only by keeping alive the spirit of free inquiry that the indispensable minimum of progress can be achieved.

Certain mental habits are commonly instilled by those who are engaged in educating: obedience and discipline, ruthlessness in the struggle for worldly success, contempt towards opposing groups, and an unquestioning credulity, a passive acceptance of the teacher's wisdom. All these habits are against life. Instead of obedience and discipline, we ought to aim at preserving independence and impulse. Instead of ruthlessness, education should try to develop justice in thought. Instead of contempt, it ought to instil reverence, and the attempt at understanding; towards the opinions of others it ought to produce, not necessarily acquiescence, but only such opposition as is combined with imaginative apprehension and a clear realization of the grounds for opposition. Instead of credulity, the object should be to stimulate constructive doubt, the love of mental adventure, the sense of worlds to conquer by enterprise and boldness in thought. Contentment with the *status quo*, and subordination of the individual pupil to political aims, owing to the indifference to the things of the mind, are the immediate causes of these evils; but beneath these causes there is one more fundamental, the fact that education is treated as a means of acquiring power over the pupil, not as a means of nourishing his own growth. It is in this that lack of reverence shows itself; and it is only by more reverence that a fundamental reform can be effected.

Obedience and discipline are supposed to be indispensable if order is to be kept in a class, and if any instruction is to be given. To some extent this is true; but the extent is much less than it is thought to be by those who regard obedience and discipline as in themselves desirable. Obedience, the yielding of one's will to outside direction, is the counterpart of authority. Both may be necessary in certain cases. Refractory children, lunatics, and criminals may require authority, and may need to be forced to obey. But in so far as this is necessary it is a misfortune: what is to be desired is the free choice of ends with which it is not necessary to interfere. And educational reformers have shown that this is far more possible than our fathers would ever have believed.[3]

What makes obedience seem necessary in schools is the large classes and overworked teachers demanded by a false economy. Those who have no experience of teaching are incapable of imagining the expense of spirit entailed by any really living instruction. They think that teachers can reasonably be expected to work as many hours as bank clerks. Intense fatigue and irritable nerves are the result, and an absolute necessity of performing the day's task mechanically. But the task cannot be performed mechanically except by exacting obedience.

If we took education seriously, and thought it as important to keep alive the minds of children as to secure victory in war, we should conduct education quite differently: we should make sure of achieving the end, even if the expense were a hundredfold greater than it is. To many men and women a small amount of teaching is a delight, and can be done with a fresh zest and life which keeps most pupils interested without any need of discipline. The few who do not become interested might be separated from the rest, and given a different kind of instruction. A teacher ought to have only as much teaching as can be done, on most days, with actual pleasure in the work, and with an awareness of the pupil's mental needs. The result would be a relation of friendliness instead of hostility between teacher and pupil, a realization on the part of most pupils that education serves to develop their own lives and is not merely an outside imposition, interfering with play and demanding many hours of sitting still. All that is necessary to this end is a (greater expenditure of money), to secure teachers with more leisure and with a natural love of teaching.

Discipline, as it exists in schools, is very largely an evil. There is a kind of discipline which is necessary to almost all achievement, and

---

3    What Madame Montessori has achieved in the way of minimizing obedience and discipline with advantage to education is almost miraculous.

which perhaps is not sufficiently valued by those who react against the purely external discipline of traditional methods. The desirable kind of discipline is the kind that comes from within, which consists in the power of pursuing a distant object steadily, foregoing and suffering many things on the way. This involves the subordination of impulse to will, the power of a directing action by large creative desires even at moments when they are not vividly alive. Without this, no serious ambition, good or bad, can be realized, no consistent purpose can dominate. This kind of discipline is very necessary, but can only result from strong desires for ends not immediately attainable, and can only be produced by education if education fosters such desires, which it seldom does at present. Such discipline springs from one's own will, not from outside authority. It is not this kind which is sought in most schools, and it is not this kind which seems to me an evil.

Although elementary education encourages the undesirable discipline that consists in passive obedience, and although hardly any existing education encourages the moral discipline of consistent self-direction, there is a certain kind of purely mental discipline which is produced by the traditional higher education. The kind I mean is that which enables a man to concentrate his thoughts at will upon any matter that he has occasion to consider, regardless of preoccupations or boredom or intellectual difficulty. This quality, though it has no important intrinsic excellence, greatly enhances the efficiency of the mind as an instrument. It is this that enables a lawyer to master the scientific details of a patent case which he forgets as soon as judgment has been given, or a civil servant to deal quickly with many different administrative questions in succession. It is this that enables men to forget private cares during business hours. In a complicated world it is a very necessary faculty for those whose work requires mental concentration.

Success in producing mental discipline is the chief merit of traditional higher education. I doubt whether it can be achieved except by compelling or persuading active attention to a prescribed task. It is for this reason chiefly that I do not believe methods such as Madame Montessori's applicable when the age of childhood has been passed. The essence of her method consists in giving a choice of occupations, any one of which is interesting to most children, and all of which are instructive. The child's attention is wholly spontaneous, as in play; it enjoys acquiring knowledge in this way, and does not acquire any knowledge which it does not desire. I am convinced that this is the best method of education with young children: the actual results make it almost impossible to think otherwise. But it is difficult to see how this method can lead to control of attention by the will. Many things which must be thought about are uninteresting, and even those that are interesting at first often become very wearisome before they have been considered as long as is necessary. The power of giving prolonged attention is very important, and it is hardly to be widely acquired except as a habit induced originally by outside pressure. Some few boys, it is true, have sufficiently strong intellectual desires to be willing to undergo all that is necessary by their own initiative and free will; but for all others an external inducement is required in order to make them learn any subject thoroughly. There is among educational reformers a certain fear of demanding great efforts, and in the world at large a growing unwillingness to be bored. Both these tendencies have their good sides, but both also have their dangers. The mental discipline which is jeopardized can be preserved by mere advice without external compulsion whenever a boy's intellectual interest and ambition can be sufficiently stimulated. A good teacher ought to be able to do this for any boy who is capable of much mental achievement; and for many of the others the present purely bookish education is probably not the best. In this way, so long as the importance of mental discipline is realized, it can probably be attained, whenever it is attainable, by appealing to the pupil's consciousness of his own needs. So long as teachers are not expected to succeed by this method, it is easy for them to slip into a slothful dullness, and blame their pupils when the fault is really their own.

Ruthlessness in the economic struggle will almost unavoidably be taught in schools so long as the economic structure of society remains unchanged. This must be particularly the case in middle-class schools, which depend for their numbers upon the good opinion of parents, and secure the good opinion of parents by advertising the successes of pupils. This is one of many ways in which the competitive organization of the State is harmful. Spontaneous and disinterested desire for knowledge is not at all uncommon in the young, and might be easily aroused in many in whom it remains latent. But it is remorselessly checked by teachers who think only of examinations, diplomas, and degrees. For the abler boys there is no time for thought, no time for the indulgence of intellectual taste, from the moment of first going to school until the moment of leaving the university. From first to last there is nothing but one long drudgery of examination tips and textbook facts. The most intelligent, at the end, are disgusted with learning, longing only to forget it and to escape into a life of action. Yet there, as before, the economic machine holds them prisoners, and all their spontaneous desires are bruised and thwarted.

The examination system, and the fact that instruction is treated mainly as training for a livelihood, leads the young to regard knowledge, from a purely utilitarian point of view, as the road to money, not as the gateway to wisdom. This would not matter so much if it affected only those who have no genuine intellectual interests. But unfortunately it affects most those whose intellectual interests are strongest, since it is upon them that the pressure of examinations falls with most severity. To them most, but to all in some degree, education appears as a means of acquiring superiority over others; it is infected through and through with ruthlessness and glorification of social inequality. Any free, disinterested consideration shows that, whatever inequalities might remain in a Utopia, the actual inequalities are almost all contrary to justice. But our educational system tends to conceal this from all except the failures, since those who succeed are on the way to profit by the inequalities, with every encouragement from the men who have directed their education.

Passive acceptance of the teacher's wisdom is easy to most boys and girls. It involves no effort of independent thought, and seems rational because the teacher knows more than his pupils; it is moreover the way to win the favor of the teacher unless he is a very exceptional man. Yet the habit of passive acceptance is a disastrous one in later life. It causes men to seek a leader, and to accept as a leader whoever is established in that position. It makes the power of Churches, Governments, party caucuses, and all the other organizations by which plain men are misled into supporting old systems which are harmful to the nation and to themselves. It is possible that there would not be much independence of thought even if education did everything to promote it; but there would certainly be more than there is at present. If the object were to make pupils think, rather than to make them accept certain conclusions, education would be conducted quite differently: there would be less rapidity of instruction and more discussion, more occasions when pupils were encouraged to express themselves, more attempt to make education concern itself with matters in which the pupils felt some interest.

Above all, there would be an endeavor to rouse and stimulate the love of mental adventure. The world in which we live is various and astonishing: some of the things that seem plainest grow more and more difficult the more they are considered; other things, which might have been thought quite impossible to discover, have nevertheless been laid bare by genius and industry. The powers of thought, the vast regions which it can master, the much more vast regions which it can only dimly suggest to imagination, give to those whose minds have traveled beyond the daily round an amazing richness of material, an escape from the triviality and wearisomeness of familiar routine, by which the whole of life is filled with interest, and the prison walls of the commonplace are broken down. The same love of adventure which takes men to the South Pole, the same passion for a conclusive trial of strength which leads some men to welcome war, can find in creative thought an outlet which is neither wasteful nor cruel, but increases the dignity of man by incarnating in life some of that shining splendor which the human spirit is bringing down out of the unknown. To give this joy, in a greater or less measure, to all who are capable of it, is the supreme end for which the education of the mind is to be valued.

It will be said that the joy of mental adventure must be rare, that there are few who can appreciate it, and that ordinary education can take no account of so aristocratic a good. I do not believe this. The joy of mental adventure is far commoner in the young than in grown men and women. Among children it is very common, and grows naturally out of the period of make-believe and fancy. It is rare in later life because everything is done to kill it during education. Men fear thought as they fear nothing else on earth—more than ruin, more even than death. Thought is subversive and revolutionary, destructive and terrible; thought is merciless to privilege, established institutions, and comfortable habits; thought is anarchic and lawless, indifferent to authority, careless of the well-tried wisdom of the ages. Thought looks into the pit of hell and is not afraid. It sees man, a feeble speck, surrounded by unfathomable depths of silence; yet it bears itself proudly, as unmoved as if it were lord of the universe. Thought is great and swift and free, the light of the world, and the chief glory of man.

But if thought is to become the possession of many, not the privilege of the few, we must have done with fear. It is fear that holds men back—fear lest their cherished beliefs should prove delusions, fear lest the institutions by which they live should prove harmful, fear lest they themselves should prove less worthy of respect than they have supposed themselves to be. "Should the working man think freely about property? Then what will become of us, the rich? Should young men and young women think freely about sex? Then what will become of morality? Should soldiers think freely about war? Then what will become of military discipline? Away with thought! Back into the shades of prejudice, lest property, morals, and war should be endangered! Better men should be stupid, slothful, and oppressive than that their thoughts should be free. For if their thoughts were free they might not think as we do. And at all costs this disaster must be averted." So the opponents of thought argue in the unconscious depths of their souls. And so they act in their churches, their schools, and their universities.

No institution inspired by fear can further life. Hope, not fear, is the creative principle in human affairs. All that has made man great has sprung from the attempt to secure what is good, not from the struggle to avert what was thought evil. It is because modern education is so seldom inspired by a great hope that it so seldom achieves a great result. The wish to preserve the past rather than the hope of creating the future dominates the minds of those who control the teaching of the young. Education should not aim at a passive awareness of dead facts, but at an activity directed towards the world that our efforts are to create. It should be inspired, not by a regretful hankering after the extinct beauties of Greece and the Renaissance, but by a shining vision of the society that is to be, of the triumphs that thought will achieve in the time to come, and of the ever-widening horizon of man's survey over the universe. Those who are taught in this spirit will be filled with life and hope and joy, able to bear their part in bringing to mankind a future less somber than the past, with faith in the glory that human effort can create.

# VI

## MARRIAGE AND THE POPULATION QUESTION

THE INFLUENCE OF the Christian religion on daily life has decayed very rapidly throughout Europe during the last hundred years. Not only has the proportion of nominal believers declined, but even among those who believe the intensity and dogmatism of belief is enormously diminished. But there is one social institution which is still profoundly affected by the Christian tradition—I mean the institution of marriage. The law and public opinion as regards marriage are dominated even now to a very great extent by the teachings of the Church, which continue to influence in this way the lives of men, women, and children in their most intimate concerns.

It is marriage as a political institution that I wish to consider, not marriage as a matter for the private morality of each individual. Marriage is regulated by law, and is regarded as a matter in which the community has a right to interfere. It is only the action of the community in regard to marriage that I am concerned to discuss: whether the present action furthers the life of the community, and if not, in what ways it ought to be changed.

There are two questions to be asked in regard to any marriage system: first, how it affects the development and character of the men and women concerned; secondly, what is its influence on the propagation and education of children. These two questions are entirely distinct, and a system may well be desirable from one of these two points of view when it is very undesirable from the other. I propose first to describe the present English law and public opinion and practice in regard to the relations of the sexes, then to consider their effects as regards children, and finally to consider how these effects, which are bad, could be obviated by a system which would also have a better influence on the character and development of men and women.

The law in England is based upon the expectation that the great majority of marriages will be lifelong. A marriage can only be dissolved if either the wife or the husband, but not both, can be proved to have committed adultery. In case the husband is the "guilty party," he must also be guilty of cruelty or desertion. Even when these conditions are fulfilled, in practice only the well-to-do can be divorced, because the expense is very great.[1] A marriage cannot be dissolved for insanity or crime, or for cruelty, however abominable, or for desertion, or for adultery by both parties; and it cannot be dissolved for any cause whatever if both husband and wife have agreed that they wish it dissolved. In all these cases the law regards the man and woman as bound together for life. A special official, the King's Proctor, is employed to prevent divorce when there is collusion and when both parties have committed adultery.[2]

---

1   There was a provision for suits *in forma pauperis*, but for various reasons this provision was nearly useless; a new and somewhat better provision has recently been made, but is still very far from satisfactory.

2   The following letter (*New Statesman*, December 4, 1915) illustrates the nature of his activities:—

DIVORCE AND WAR.

*To the Editor of the* "New Statesman."

SIR,—The following episodes may be of interest to your readers. Under the new facilities for divorce offered to the London poor, a poor woman recently obtained a decree *nisi* for divorce against her husband, who had often covered her body with bruises, infected her with a dangerous disease, and committed bigamy. By this bigamous marriage the husband had ten illegitimate children. In order to prevent this decree being made absolute, the Treasury spent at least £200 of the taxes in briefing a leading counsel and an eminent junior counsel and in bringing about ten witnesses from a city a hundred miles away to prove that this woman had committed casual acts of adultery in 1895 and 1898. The net result is that this woman will probably be forced by destitution into further adultery, and that the husband will be able to treat his mistress exactly as he treated his wife, with impunity, so far as disease is concerned. In nearly every other civilized country the marriage would have been dissolved, the children could have been legitimated by subsequent marriage, and the lawyers employed by the Treasury would not have earned the large fees they did from the community for an achievement which seems to most other lawyers thoroughly anti-social in its effects. If any lawyers really feel that society is benefited by this sort of litigation, why cannot they give their services for nothing, like the lawyers who assisted the wife? If we are to practise economy in war-time, why cannot the King's Proctor be satisfied with a junior counsel only? The fact remains that many persons situated like the husband and wife in question prefer to avoid having illegitimate children, and the birth-rate accordingly suffers.

The other episode is this. A divorce was obtained by Mr. A. against Mrs. A. and Mr. B. Mr. B. was married and Mrs. B., on hearing of the divorce proceedings, obtained a decree nisi against Mr. B. Mr. B. is at any moment liable to be called to the Front, but Mrs. B. has for some months declined to make the decree *nisi* absolute, and this prevents him marrying Mrs. A., as he feels in honor bound to do. Yet the law allows any petitioner, male or female, to obtain a decree *nisi* and to refrain from

This interesting system embodies the opinions held by the Church of England some fifty years ago, and by most Nonconformists then and now. It rests upon the assumption that adultery is sin, and that when this sin has been committed by one party to the marriage, the other is entitled to revenge if he is rich. But when both have committed the same sin, or when the one who has not committed it feels no righteous anger, the right to revenge does not exist. As soon as this point of view is understood, the law, which at first seems somewhat strange, is seen to be perfectly consistent. It rests, broadly speaking, upon four propositions: (1) that sexual intercourse outside marriage is sin; (2) that resentment of adultery by the "innocent" party is a righteous horror of wrong-doing; (3) that his resentment, but nothing else, may be rightly regarded as making a common life impossible; (4) that the poor have no right to fine feelings. The Church of England, under the influence of the High Church, has ceased to believe the third of these propositions, but it still believes the first and second, and does nothing actively to show that it disbelieves the fourth.

The penalty for infringing the marriage law is partly financial, but depends mainly upon public opinion. A rather small section of the public genuinely believes that sexual relations outside marriage are wicked; those who believe this are naturally kept in ignorance of the conduct of friends who feel otherwise, and are able to go through life not knowing how others live or what others think. This small section of the public regards as depraved not only actions, but opinions, which are contrary to its principles. It is able to control the professions of politicians through its influence on elections, and the votes of the House of Lords through the presence of the Bishops. By these means it governs legislation, and makes any change in the marriage law almost impossible. It is able, also, to secure in most cases that a man who openly infringes the marriage law shall be dismissed from

---

making it absolute for motives which are probably discreditable. The Divorce Law Commissioners strongly condemned this state of things, and the hardship in question is immensely aggravated in war-time, just as the war has given rise to many cases of bigamy owing to the chivalrous desire of our soldiers to obtain for the *de facto* wife and family the separation allowance of the State. The legal wife is often united by similar ties to another man. I commend these facts to consideration in your columns, having regard to your frequent complaints of a falling birth-rate. The iniquity of our marriage laws is an important contributory cause to the fall in question.

Yours, etc.,

E. S. P. HAYNES.

*November 29th.*

his employment or ruined by the defection of his customers or clients. A doctor or lawyer, or a tradesman in a country town, cannot make a living, nor can a politician be in Parliament, if he is publicly known to be "immoral." Whatever a man's own conduct may be, he is not likely to defend publicly those who have been branded, lest some of the odium should fall on him. Yet so long as a man has not been branded, few men will object to him, whatever they may know privately of his behavior in these respects.

Owing to the nature of the penalty, it falls very unequally upon different professions. An actor or journalist usually escapes all punishment. An urban workingman can almost always do as he likes. A man of private means, unless he wishes to take part in public life, need not suffer at all if he has chosen his friends suitably. Women, who formerly suffered more than men, now suffer less, since there are large circles in which no social penalty is inflicted, and a very rapidly increasing number of women who do not believe the conventional code. But for the majority of men outside the working classes the penalty is still sufficiently severe to be prohibitive.

The result of this state of things is a widespread but very flimsy hypocrisy, which allows many infractions of the code, and forbids only those which must become public. A man may not live openly with a woman who is not his wife, an unmarried woman may not have a child, and neither man nor woman may get into the divorce court. Subject to these restrictions, there is in practice very great freedom. It is this practical freedom which makes the state of the law seem tolerable to those who do not accept the principles upon which it is based. What has to be sacrificed to propitiate the holders of strict views is not pleasure, but only children and a common life and truth and honesty. It cannot be supposed that this is the result desired by those who maintain the code, but equally it cannot be denied that this is the result which they do in fact achieve. Extra-matrimonial relations which do not lead to children and are accompanied by a certain amount of deceit remain unpunished, but severe penalties fall on those which are honest or lead to children.

Within marriage, the expense of children leads to continually greater limitation of families. The limitation is greatest among those who have most sense of parental responsibility and most wish to educate their children well, since it is to them that the expense of children is most severe. But although the economic motive for limiting families has hitherto probably been the strongest, it is being continually reinforced by another. Women are acquiring freedom—not merely outward and formal freedom, but inward freedom, enabling them to think and feel genuinely, not according to received maxims. To the men who have prated confidently of women's natural instincts, the result would be surprising if they were aware of it. Very large numbers of women, when they are sufficiently free to think for themselves, do not desire to have children, or at most desire one child in order not to miss the experience which a child brings. There are women who are intelligent and active-minded who resent the slavery to the body which is involved in having children. There are ambitious women, who desire a career which leaves no time for children. There are women who love pleasure and gaiety, and women who love the admiration of men; such women will at least postpone child-bearing until their youth is past. All these classes of women are rapidly becoming more numerous, and it may be safely assumed that their numbers will continue to increase for many years to come.

It is too soon to judge with any confidence as to the effects of women's freedom upon private life and upon the life of the nation. But I think it is not too soon to see that it will be profoundly different from the effect expected by the pioneers of the women's movement. Men have invented, and women in the past have often accepted, a theory that women are the guardians of the race, that their life centers in motherhood, that all their instincts and desires are directed, consciously or unconsciously, to this end. Tolstoy's Natacha illustrates this theory: she is charming, gay, liable to passion, until she is married; then she becomes merely a virtuous mother, without any mental life. This result has Tolstoy's entire approval. It must be admitted that it is very desirable from the point of view of the nation, whatever we may think of it in relation to private life. It must also be admitted that it is probably common among women who are physically vigorous and not highly civilized. But in countries like France and England it is becoming increasingly rare. More and more women find motherhood unsatisfying, not what their needs demand. And more and more there comes to be a conflict between their personal development and the future of the community. It is difficult to know what ought to be done to mitigate this conflict, but I think it is worth while to see what are likely to be its effects if it is not mitigated.

Owing to the combination of economic prudence with the increasing freedom of women, there is at present a selective birth-rate of a very singular kind.[3] In France the population is practically stationary, and in England it is rapidly becoming so; this means that some sections are dwindling while others are increasing. Unless some change occurs, the sections that are dwindling will practically become extinct, and the population will be almost wholly replenished from the sections that are now increasing.[4] The sections that are dwindling include the whole middle-class and the skilled artisans. The sections that are increasing are the very poor, the shiftless and drunken, the feeble-minded—feeble-minded women, especially, are apt to be very prolific. There is an increase in those sections of the population which still actively believe the Catholic religion, such as the Irish and the Bretons, because the Catholic religion forbids limitation of families. Within the classes that are dwindling, it is the best elements that are dwindling most rapidly. Working-class boys of exceptional ability rise, by means of scholarships, into the professional class; they naturally desire to marry into the class to which they belong by education, not into the class from which they spring; but as they have no money beyond what they earn, they cannot marry young, or afford a large family. The result is that in each generation the best elements are extracted from the working classes and artificially sterilized, at least in comparison with those who are left. In the professional classes the young women who have initiative, energy, or intelligence are as a rule not inclined to marry young, or to have more than one or two children when they do marry. Marriage has been in the past the only obvious means of livelihood for women; pressure from parents and fear of becoming an old maid combined to force many women to marry in spite of a complete absence of inclination for the duties of a wife. But now a young woman of ordinary intelligence can easily earn her own living, and can acquire freedom and experience without the permanent ties of a husband and a family of children. The result is that if she marries she marries late.

For these reasons, if an average sample of children were taken out of

---

3   Some interesting facts were given by Mr. Sidney Webb in two letters to The Times, October 11 and 16, 1906; there is also a Fabian tract on the subject: "The Decline in the Birth-Rate," by Sidney Webb (No. 131). Some further information may be found in "The Declining Birth-Rate: Its National and International Significance," by A. Newsholme, M.D., M.R.C.S. (Cassell, 1911).

4   The fall in the death-rate, and especially in the infant mortality, which has occurred concurrently with the fall in the birth-rate, has hitherto been sufficiently great to allow the population of Great Britain to go on increasing. But there are obvious limits to the fall of the death-rate, whereas the birth-rate might easily fall to a point which would make an actual diminution of numbers unavoidable.

the population of England, and their parents were examined, it would be found that prudence, energy, intellect, and enlightenment were less common among the parents than in the population in general; while shiftlessness, feeble-mindedness, stupidity, and superstition were more common than in the population in general. It would be found that those who are prudent or energetic or intelligent or enlightened actually fail to reproduce their own numbers; that is to say, they do not on the average have as many as two children each who survive infancy. On the other hand, those who have the opposite qualities have, on the average, more than two children each, and more than reproduce their own numbers.

It is impossible to estimate the effect which this will have upon the character of the population without a much greater knowledge of heredity than exists at present. But so long as children continue to live with their parents, parental example and early education must have a great influence in developing their character, even if we leave heredity entirely out of account. Whatever may be thought of genius, there can be no doubt that intelligence, whether through heredity or through education, tends to run in families, and that the decay of the families in which it is common must lower the mental standard of the population. It seems unquestionable that if our economic system and our moral standards remain unchanged, there will be, in the next two or three generations, a rapid change for the worse in the character of the population in all civilized countries, and an actual diminution of numbers in the most civilized.

The diminution of numbers, in all likelihood, will rectify itself in time through the elimination of those characteristics which at present lead to a small birth-rate. Men and women who can still believe the Catholic faith will have a biological advantage; gradually a race will grow up which will be impervious to all the assaults of reason, and will believe imperturbably that limitation of families leads to hell-fire. Women who have mental interests, who care about art or literature or politics, who desire a career or who value their liberty, will gradually grow rarer, and be more and more replaced by a placid maternal type which has no interests outside the home and no dislike of the burden of motherhood. This result, which ages of masculine domination have vainly striven to achieve, is likely to be the final outcome of women's emancipation and of their attempt to enter upon a wider sphere than that to which the jealousy of men confined them in the past.

Perhaps, if the facts could be ascertained, it would be found that something of the same kind occurred in the Roman Empire. The decay of energy and intelligence during the second, third, and fourth centuries of our era has always remained more or less mysterious. But there is reason to think that then, as now, the best elements of the population in each generation failed to reproduce themselves, and that the least vigorous were, as a rule, those to whom the continuance of the race was due. One might be tempted to suppose that civilization, when it has reached a certain height, becomes unstable, and tends to decay through some inherent weakness, some failure to adapt the life of instinct to the intense mental life of a period of high culture. But such vague theories have always something glib and superstitious which makes them worthless as scientific explanations or as guides to action. It is not by a literary formula, but by detailed and complex thought, that a true solution is to be found.

Let us first be clear as to what we desire. There is no importance in an increasing population; on the contrary, if the population of Europe were stationary, it would be much easier to promote economic reform and to avoid war. What is regrettable *at present* is not the decline of the birth-rate in itself, but the fact that the decline is greatest in the best elements of the population. There is reason, however, to fear in the future three bad results: first, an absolute decline in the numbers of English, French, and Germans; secondly, as a consequence of this decline, their subjugation by less civilized races and the extinction of their tradition; thirdly, a revival of their numbers on a much lower plane of civilization, after generations of selection of those who have neither intelligence nor foresight. If this result is to be avoided, the present unfortunate selectiveness of the birth-rate must be somehow stopped.

The problem is one which applies to the whole of Western civilization. There is no difficulty in discovering a theoretical solution, but there is great difficulty in persuading men to adopt a solution in practice, because the effects to be feared are not immediate and the subject is one upon which people are not in the habit of using their reason. If a rational solution is ever adopted, the cause will probably be international rivalry. It is obvious that if one State—say Germany—adopted a rational means of dealing with the matter, it would acquire an enormous advantage over other States unless they did likewise. After the war, it is possible that population questions will attract more attention than they did before, and it is likely that they will be studied from the point of view of international rivalry. This motive, unlike reason and humanity, is perhaps strong enough to overcome men's objections to a scientific treatment of the birth-rate.

In the past, at most periods and in most societies, the instincts of men and women led of themselves to a more than sufficient birth-rate; Malthus's statement of the population question had been true enough up to the time when he wrote. It is still true of barbarous and semi-civilized races, and of the worst elements among civilized races. But it has become false as regards the more civilized half of the population in Western Europe and America. Among them, instinct no longer suffices to keep numbers even stationary.

We may sum up the reasons for this in order of importance, as follows:—

1. The expense of children is very great if parents are conscientious.

2. An increasing number of women desire to have no children, or only one or two, in order not to be hampered in their own careers.

3. Owing to the excess of women, a large number of women remain unmarried. These women, though not debarred in practice from relations with men, are debarred by the code from having children. In this class are to be found an enormous and increasing number of women who earn their own living as typists, in shops, or otherwise. The war has opened many employments to women from which they were formerly excluded, and this change is probably only in part temporary.

If the sterilizing of the best parts of the population is to be arrested, the first and most pressing necessity is the removal of the economic motives for limiting families. The expense of children ought to be borne wholly by the community. Their food and clothing and education ought to be provided, not only to the very poor as a matter of charity, but to all classes as a matter of public interest. In addition to this, a woman who is capable of earning money, and who abandons wage-earning for motherhood, ought to receive from the State as nearly as possible what she would have received if she had not had children. The only condition attached to State maintenance of the mother and the children should be that both parents are physically and mentally sound in all ways likely to affect the children. Those who are not sound should not be debarred from having children, but should continue, as at present, to bear the expense of children themselves.

It ought to be recognized that the law is only concerned with marriage through the question of children, and should be indifferent to what is called "morality," which is based upon custom and texts of the Bible, not upon any real consideration of the needs of the community.

The excess women, who at present are in every way discouraged from having children, ought no longer to be discouraged. If the State is to undertake the expense of children, it has the right, on eugenic grounds, to know who the father is, and to demand a certain stability in a union. But there is no reason to demand or expect a lifelong stability, or to exact any ground for divorce beyond mutual consent. This would make it possible for the women who must at present remain unmarried to have children if they wished it. In this way an enormous and unnecessary waste would be prevented, and a great deal of needless unhappiness would be avoided.

There is no necessity to begin such a system all at once. It might be begun tentatively with certain exceptionally desirable sections of the community. It might then be extended gradually, with the experience of its working which had been derived from the first experiment. If the birth-rate were very much increased, the eugenic conditions exacted might be made more strict.

There are of course various practical difficulties in the way of such a scheme: the opposition of the Church and the upholders of traditional morality, the fear of weakening parental responsibility, and the expense. All these, however, might be overcome. But there remains one difficulty which it seems impossible to overcome completely in England, and that is, that the whole conception is anti-democratic, since it regards some men as better than others, and would demand that the State should bestow a better education upon the children of some men than upon the children of others. This is contrary to all the principles of progressive politics in England. For this reason it can hardly be expected that any such method of dealing with the population question will ever be adopted in its entirety in this country. Something of the sort may well be done in Germany, and if so, it will assure German hegemony as no merely military victory could do. But among ourselves we can only hope to see it adopted in some partial, piecemeal fashion, and probably only after a change in the economic structure of society which will remove most of the artificial inequalities that progressive parties are rightly trying to diminish.

So far we have been considering the question of the reproduction of the race, rather than the effect of sex relations in fostering or hindering the development of men and women. From the point of view of the race, what seems needed is a complete removal of the economic burdens due to children from all parents who are not physically or mentally unfit, and as much freedom in the law as is compatible with public knowledge of paternity. Exactly the same changes seem called for when the question is considered from the point of view of the men and women concerned.

In regard to marriage, as with all the other traditional bonds between human beings, a very extraordinary change is taking place, wholly inevitable, wholly necessary as a stage in the development of a new life, but by no means wholly satisfactory until it is completed. All the traditional bonds were based on *authority*—of the king, the feudal baron, the priest, the father, the husband. All these bonds, just because they were based on authority, are dissolving or already dissolved, and the creation of other bonds to take their place is as yet very incomplete. For this reason human relations have at present an unusual triviality, and do less than they did formerly to break down the hard walls of the Ego.

The ideal of marriage in the past depended upon the authority of the husband, which was admitted as a right by the wife. The husband was free, the wife was a willing slave. In all matters which concerned husband and wife jointly, it was taken for granted that the husband's fiat should be final. The wife was expected to be faithful, while the husband, except in very religious societies, was only expected to throw a decent veil over his infidelities. Families could not be limited except by continence, and a wife had no recognized right to demand continence, however she might suffer from frequent children.

So long as the husband's right to authority was unquestioningly believed by both men and women, this system was fairly satisfactory, and afforded to both a certain instinctive fulfilment which is rarely achieved among educated people now. Only one will, the husband's, had to be taken into account, and there was no need of the difficult adjustments required when common decisions have to be reached by two equal wills. The wife's desires were not treated seriously enough to enable them to thwart the husband's needs, and the wife herself, unless she was exceptionally selfish, did not seek self-development, or see in marriage anything but an opportunity for duties. Since she did not seek or expect much happiness, she suffered less, when happiness was not attained, than a woman does now: her suffering contained no element of indignation or surprise, and did not readily turn into bitterness and sense of injury.

The saintly, self-sacrificing woman whom our ancestors praised had her place in a certain organic conception of society, the conception of the ordered hierarchy of authorities which dominated the Middle

Ages. She belongs to the same order of ideas as the faithful servant, the loyal subject, and the orthodox son of the Church. This whole order of ideas has vanished from the civilized world, and it is to be hoped that it has vanished for ever, in spite of the fact that the society which it produced was vital and in some ways full of nobility. The old order has been destroyed by the new ideals of justice and liberty, beginning with religion, passing on to politics, and reaching at last the private relations of marriage and the family. When once the question has been asked, "Why should a woman submit to a man?" when once the answers derived from tradition and the Bible have ceased to satisfy, there is no longer any possibility of maintaining the old subordination. To every man who has the power of thinking impersonally and freely, it is obvious, as soon as the question is asked, that the rights of women are precisely the same as the rights of men. Whatever dangers and difficulties, whatever temporary chaos, may be incurred in the transition to equality, the claims of reason are so insistent and so clear that no opposition to them can hope to be long successful.

Mutual liberty, which is now demanded, is making the old form of marriage impossible. But a new form, which shall be an equally good vehicle for instinct, and an equal help to spiritual growth, has not yet been developed. For the present, women who are conscious of liberty as something to be preserved are also conscious of the difficulty of preserving it. The wish for mastery is an ingredient in most men's sexual passions, especially in those which are strong and serious. It survives in many men whose theories are entirely opposed to despotism. The result is a fight for liberty on the one side and for life on the other. Women feel that they must protect their individuality; men feel, often very dumbly, that the repression of instinct which is demanded of them is incompatible with vigor and initiative. The clash of these opposing moods makes all real mingling of personalities impossible; the man and woman remain hard, separate units, continually asking themselves whether anything of value to themselves is resulting from the union. The effect is that relations tend to become trivial and temporary, a pleasure rather than the satisfaction of a profound need, an excitement, not an attainment. The fundamental loneliness into which we are born remains untouched, and the hunger for inner companionship remains unappeased.

No cheap and easy solution of this trouble is possible. It is a trouble which affects most the most civilized men and women, and is an outcome of the increasing sense of individuality which springs inevitably from mental progress. I doubt if there is any radical cure except in some form of religion, so firmly and sincerely believed as to dominate even the life of instinct. The individual is not the end and aim of his own being: outside the individual, there is the community, the future of mankind, the immensity of the universe in which all our hopes and fears are a mere pin-point. A man and woman with reverence for the spirit of life in each other, with an equal sense of their own unimportance beside the whole life of man, may become comrades without interference with liberty, and may achieve the union of instinct without doing violence to the life of mind and spirit. As religion dominated the old form of marriage, so religion must dominate the new. But it must be a new religion, based upon liberty, justice, and love, not upon authority and law and hell-fire.

A bad effect upon the relations of men and women has been produced by the romantic movement, through directing attention to what ought to be an incidental good, not the purpose for which relations exist. Love is what gives intrinsic value to a marriage, and, like art and thought, it is one of the supreme things which make human life worth preserving. But though there is no good marriage without love, the best marriages have a purpose which goes beyond love. The love of two people for each other is too circumscribed, too separate from the community, to be by itself the main purpose of a good life. It is not in itself a sufficient source of activities, it is not sufficiently prospective, to make an existence in which ultimate satisfaction can be found. It brings its great moments, and then its times which are less great, which are unsatisfying because they are less great. It becomes, sooner or later, retrospective, a tomb of dead joys, not a well-spring of new life. This evil is inseparable from any purpose which is to be achieved in a single supreme emotion. The only adequate purposes are those which stretch out into the future, which can never be fully achieved, but are always growing, and infinite with the infinity of human endeavor. And it is only when love is linked to some infinite purpose of this kind that it can have the seriousness and depth of which it is capable.

For the great majority of men and women seriousness in sex relations is most likely to be achieved through children. Children are to most people rather a need than a desire: instinct is as a rule only consciously directed towards what used to lead to children. The desire for children is apt to develop in middle life, when the adventure of one's own existence is past, when the friendships of youth seem less important than they once did, when the prospect of a lonely old age begins to terrify, and the feeling of having no share in the future becomes oppressive. Then those who, while they were young, have had no sense that children would be a fulfilment of their needs, begin to regret their former contempt for the normal, and to envy acquaintances whom before they had thought humdrum. But owing to economic causes it is often impossible for the young, and especially for the best of the young, to have children without sacrificing things of vital importance to their own lives. And so youth passes, and the need is felt too late.

Needs without corresponding desires have grown increasingly common as life has grown more different from that primitive existence from which our instincts are derived, and to which, rather than to that of the present day, they are still very largely adapted. An unsatisfied need produces, in the end, as much pain and as much distortion of character as if it had been associated with a conscious desire. For this reason, as well as for the sake of the race, it is important to remove the present economic inducements to childlessness. There is no necessity whatever to urge parenthood upon those who feel disinclined to it, but there is necessity not to place obstacles in the way of those who have no such disinclination.

In speaking of the importance of preserving seriousness in the relations of men and women, I do not mean to suggest that relations which are not serious are always harmful. Traditional morality has erred by laying stress on what ought not to happen, rather than on what ought to happen. What is important is that men and women should find, sooner or later, the best relation of which their natures are capable. It is not always possible to know in advance what will be the best, or to be sure of not missing the best if everything that can be doubted is rejected. Among primitive races, a man wants a female, a woman wants a male, and there is no such differentiation as makes one a much more suitable companion than another. But with the increasing complexity of disposition that civilized life brings, it becomes more and more difficult to find the man or woman who will bring happiness, and more and more necessary to make it not too difficult to acknowledge a mistake.

The present marriage law is an inheritance from a simpler age, and is supported, in the main, by unreasoning fears and by contempt for all that is delicate and difficult in the life of the mind. Owing to the law, large numbers of men and women are condemned, so far as their ostensible relations are concerned, to the society of an utterly uncongenial companion, with all the embittering consciousness that escape is practically impossible. In these circumstances, happier relations with others are often sought, but they have to be clandestine, without a common life, and without children. Apart from the great evil of being clandestine, such relations have some almost inevitable drawbacks. They are liable to emphasize sex unduly, to be exciting and disturbing; and it is hardly possible that they should bring a real satisfaction of instinct. It is the combination of love, children, and a common life that makes the best relation between a man and a woman. The law at present confines children and a common life within the bonds of monogamy, but it cannot confine love. By forcing many to separate love from children and a common life, the law cramps their lives, prevents them from reaching the full measure of their possible development, and inflicts a wholly unnecessary torture upon those who are not content to become frivolous.

To sum up: The present state of the law, of public opinion, and of our economic system is tending to degrade the quality of the race, by making the worst half of the population the parents of more than half of the next generation. At the same time, women's claim to liberty is making the old form of marriage a hindrance to the development of both men and women. A new system is required, if the European nations are not to degenerate, and if the relations of men and women are to have the strong happiness and organic seriousness which belonged to the best marriages in the past. The new system must be based upon the fact that to produce children is a service to the State, and ought not to expose parents to heavy pecuniary penalties. It will have to recognize that neither the law nor public opinion should concern itself with the private relations of men and women, except where children are concerned. It ought to remove the inducements to make relations clandestine and childless. It ought to admit that, although lifelong monogamy is best when it is successful, the increasing complexity of our needs makes it increasingly often a failure for which divorce is the best preventive. Here, as elsewhere, liberty is the basis of political wisdom. And when liberty has been won, what remains to be desired must be left to the conscience and religion of individual men and women.

# VII

## RELIGION AND THE CHURCHES

ALMOST ALL THE changes which the world has undergone since the end of the Middle Ages are due to the discovery and diffusion of new knowledge. This was the primary cause of the Renaissance, the Reformation, and the industrial revolution. It was also, very directly, the cause of the decay of dogmatic religion. The study of classical texts and early Church history, Copernican astronomy and physics, Darwinian biology and comparative anthropology, have each in turn battered down some part of the edifice of Catholic dogma, until, for almost all thinking and instructed people, the most that seems defensible is some inner spirit, some vague hope, and some not very definite feeling of moral obligation. This result might perhaps have remained limited to the educated minority but for the fact that the Churches have almost everywhere opposed political progress with the same bitterness with which they have opposed progress in thought. Political conservatism has brought the Churches into conflict with whatever was vigorous in the working classes, and has spread free thought in wide circles which might otherwise have remained orthodox for centuries. The decay of dogmatic religion is, for good or evil, one of the most important facts in the modern world. Its effects have hardly yet begun to show themselves: what they will be it is impossible to say, but they will certainly be profound and far-reaching.

Religion is partly personal, partly social: to the Protestant primarily personal, to the Catholic primarily social. It is only when the two elements are intimately blended that religion becomes a powerful force in molding society. The Catholic Church, as it existed from the time of Constantine to the time of the Reformation, represented a blending which would have seemed incredible if it had not been actually achieved, the blending of Christ and Cæsar, of the morality of humble submission with the pride of Imperial Rome. Those who loved the one could find it in the Thebaid; those who loved the other could admire it in the pomp of metropolitan archbishops. In St. Francis and Innocent

III the same two sides of the Church are still represented. But since the Reformation personal religion has been increasingly outside the Catholic Church, while the religion which has remained Catholic has been increasingly a matter of institutions and politics and historic continuity. This division has weakened the force of religion: religious bodies have not been strengthened by the enthusiasm and single-mindedness of the men in whom personal religion is strong, and these men have not found their teaching diffused and made permanent by the power of ecclesiastical institutions.

The Catholic Church achieved, during the Middle Ages, the most organic society and the most harmonious inner synthesis of instinct, mind, and spirit, that the Western world has ever known. St. Francis, Thomas Aquinas, and Dante represent its summit as regards individual development. The cathedrals, the mendicant Orders, and the triumph of the Papacy over the Empire represent its supreme political success. But the perfection which had been achieved was a narrow perfection: instinct, mind, and spirit all suffered from curtailment in order to fit into the pattern; laymen found themselves subject to the Church in ways which they resented, and the Church used its power for rapacity and oppression. The perfect synthesis was an enemy to new growth, and after the time of Dante all that was living in the world had first to fight for its right to live against the representatives of the old order. This fight is even now not ended. Only when it is quite ended, both in the external world of politics and in the internal world of men's own thoughts, will it be possible for a new organic society and a new inner synthesis to take the place which the Church held for a thousand years.

The clerical profession suffers from two causes, one of which it shares with some other professions, while the other is peculiar to itself. The cause peculiar to it is the convention that clergymen are more virtuous than other men. Any average selection of mankind, set apart and told that it excels the rest in virtue, must tend to sink below the average. This is an ancient commonplace in regard to princes and those who used to be called "the great." But it is no less true as regards those of the clergy who are not genuinely and by nature as much better than the average as they are conventionally supposed to be. The other source of harm to the clerical profession is endowments. Property which is only available for those who will support an established institution has a tendency to warp men's judgments as to the excellence of the institution. The tendency is aggravated when the property is associated with social consideration and opportunities for petty power. It is at its worst when the institution is tied by law to an ancient creed, almost impossible to change, and yet quite out of touch with the unfettered thought of the present day. All these causes combine to damage the moral force of the Church.

It is not so much that the creed of the Church is the wrong one. What is amiss is the mere existence of a creed. As soon as income, position, and power are dependent upon acceptance of no matter what creed, intellectual honesty is imperiled. Men will tell themselves that a formal assent is justified by the good which it will enable them to do. They fail to realize that, in those whose mental life has any vigor, loss of complete intellectual integrity puts an end to the power of doing good, by producing gradually in all directions an inability to see truth simply. The strictness of party discipline has introduced the same evil in politics; there, because the evil is comparatively new, it is visible to many who think it unimportant as regards the Church. But the evil is greater as regards the Church, because religion is of more importance than politics, and because it is more necessary that the exponents of religion should be wholly free from taint.

The evils we have been considering seem inseparable from the existence of a professional priesthood. If religion is not to be harmful in a world of rapid change, it must, like the Society of Friends, be carried on by men who have other occupations during the week, who do their religious work from enthusiasm, without receiving any payment. And such men, because they know the everyday world, are not likely to fall into a remote morality which no one regards as applicable to common life. Being free, they will not be bound to reach certain conclusions decided in advance, but will be able to consider moral and religious questions genuinely, without bias. Except in a quite stationary society, no religious life can be living or a real support to the spirit unless it is freed from the incubus of a professional priesthood.

It is largely for these reasons that so little of what is valuable in morals and religion comes nowadays from the men who are eminent in the religious world. It is true that among professed believers there are many who are wholly sincere, who feel still the inspiration which Christianity brought before it had been weakened by the progress of knowledge. These sincere believers are valuable to the world because they keep alive the conviction that the life of the spirit is what is of most importance to men and women. Some of them, in all the countries now at war, have had the courage to preach peace and love in the name of Christ, and have done what lay in their power to mitigate the bitterness of hatred. All praise is due to these men, and without them the world would be even worse than it is.

But it is not through even the most sincere and courageous believers in the traditional religion that a new spirit can come into the world. It is not through them that religion can be brought back to those who have lost it because their minds were active, not because their spirit was dead. Believers in the traditional religion necessarily look to the past for inspiration rather than to the future. They seek wisdom in the teaching of Christ, which, admirable as it is, remains quite inadequate for many of the social and spiritual issues of modern life. Art and intellect and all the problems of government are ignored in the Gospels. Those who, like Tolstoy, endeavor seriously to take the Gospels as a guide to life are compelled to regard the ignorant peasant as the best type of man, and to brush aside political questions by an extreme and impracticable anarchism.

If a religious view of life and the world is ever to reconquer the thoughts and feelings of free-minded men and women, much that we are accustomed to associate with religion will have to be discarded. The first and greatest change that is required is to establish a morality of initiative, not a morality of submission, a morality of hope rather than fear, of things to be done rather than of things to be left undone. It is not the whole duty of man to slip through the world so as to escape the wrath of God. The world is *our* world, and it rests with us to make it a heaven or a hell. The power is ours, and the kingdom and the glory would be ours also if we had courage and insight to create them. The religious life that we must seek will not be one of occasional solemnity and superstitious prohibitions, it will not be sad or ascetic, it will concern itself little with rules of conduct. It will be inspired by a vision of what human life may be, and will be happy with the joy of creation, living in a large free world of initiative and hope. It will love mankind, not for what they are to the outward eye, but for what imagination shows that they have it in them to become. It will not readily condemn, but it will give praise to positive achievement rather than negative sinlessness, to the joy of life, the quick affection, the creative insight, by which the world may grow young and beautiful and filled with vigor.

"Religion" is a word which has many meanings and a long history. In origin, it was concerned with certain rites, inherited from a remote past, performed originally for some reason long since forgotten, and associated from time to time with various myths to account for their supposed importance. Much of this lingers still. A religious man is one who goes to church, a communicant, one who "practises," as Catholics say. How he behaves otherwise, or how he feels concerning life and man's place in the world, does not bear upon the question whether he is "religious" in this simple but historically correct sense. Many men and women are religious in this sense without having in their natures anything that deserves to be called religion in the sense in which I mean the word. The mere familiarity of the Church service has made them impervious to it; they are unconscious of all the history and human experience by which the liturgy has been enriched, and unmoved by the glibly repeated words of the Gospel, which condemn almost all the activities of those who fancy themselves disciples of Christ. This fate must overtake any habitual rite: it is impossible that it should continue to produce much effect after it has been performed so often as to grow mechanical.

The activities of men may be roughly derived from three sources, not in actual fact sharply separate one from another, but sufficiently distinguishable to deserve different names. The three sources I mean are instinct, mind, and spirit, and of these three it is the life of the spirit that makes religion.

The life of instinct includes all that man shares with the lower animals, all that is concerned with self-preservation and reproduction and the desires and impulses derivative from these. It includes vanity and love of possessions, love of family, and even much of what makes love of country. It includes all the impulses that are essentially concerned with the biological success of oneself or one's group—for among gregarious animals the life of instinct includes the group. The impulses which it includes may not in fact make for success, and may often in fact militate against it, but are nevertheless those of which success is the *raison d'être*, those which express the animal nature of man and his position among a world of competitors.

The life of the mind is the life of pursuit of knowledge, from mere childish curiosity up to the greatest efforts of thought. Curiosity exists in animals, and serves an obvious biological purpose; but it is only in men that it passes beyond the investigation of particular objects which may be edible or poisonous, friendly or hostile. Curiosity is the primary impulse out of which the whole edifice of scientific knowledge has grown. Knowledge has been found so useful that most actual acquisition of it is no longer prompted by curiosity; innumerable other motives now contribute to foster the intellectual life. Nevertheless, direct love of knowledge and dislike of error still play a very large part, especially with those who are most successful in learning. No man acquires much knowledge unless the acquisition is in itself delightful to him, apart from any consciousness of the use to which the knowledge may be put. The impulse to acquire knowledge and the activities which center round it constitute what I mean by the life of the mind. The life of the mind consists of thought which is wholly or partially impersonal, in the sense that it concerns itself with objects on their own account, and not merely on account of their bearing upon our instinctive life.

The life of the spirit centers round impersonal feeling, as the life of the mind centers round impersonal thought. In this sense, all art belongs to the life of the spirit, though its greatness is derived from its being also intimately bound up with the life of instinct. Art starts from instinct and rises into the region of the spirit; religion starts from the spirit and endeavors to dominate and inform the life of instinct. It is possible to feel the same interest in the joys and sorrows of others as in our own, to love and hate independently of all relation to ourselves, to care about the destiny of man and the development of the universe without a thought that we are personally involved. Reverence and worship, the sense of an obligation to mankind, the feeling of imperativeness and acting under orders which traditional religion has interpreted as Divine inspiration, all belong to the life of the spirit. And deeper than all these lies the sense of a mystery half revealed, of a hidden wisdom and glory, of a transfiguring vision in which common things lose their solid importance and become a thin veil behind which the ultimate truth of the world is dimly seen. It is such feelings that are the source of religion, and if they were to die most of what is best would vanish out of life.

Instinct, mind, and spirit are all essential to a full life; each has its own excellence and its own corruption. Each can attain a spurious excellence at the expense of the others; each has a tendency to encroach upon the others; but in the life which is to be sought all three will be developed in coördination, and intimately blended in a single harmonious whole. Among uncivilized men instinct is supreme, and mind and spirit hardly exist. Among educated men at the present day mind is developed, as a rule, at the expense of both instinct and spirit, producing a curious inhumanity and lifelessness, a paucity of both personal and impersonal desires, which leads to cynicism and intellectual destructiveness. Among ascetics and most of those who would be called saints, the life of the spirit has been developed at the expense of instinct and mind, producing an outlook which is impossible to those who have a healthy animal life and to those who have a love of active thought. It is not in any of these one-sided developments that we can find wisdom or a philosophy which will bring new life to the civilized world.

Among civilized men and women at the present day it is rare to find instinct, mind, and spirit in harmony. Very few have achieved a practical philosophy which gives its due place to each; as a rule, instinct is at war with either mind or spirit, and mind and spirit are at war with each other. This strife compels men and women to direct much of their energy inwards, instead of being able to expend it all in objective activities. When a man achieves a precarious inward peace by the defeat of a part of his nature, his vital force is impaired, and his growth is no longer quite healthy. If men are to remain whole, it is very necessary that they should achieve a reconciliation of instinct, mind, and spirit.

Instinct is the source of vitality, the bond that unites the life of the individual with the life of the race, the basis of all profound sense of union with others, and the means by which the collective life nourishes the life of the separate units. But instinct by itself leaves us powerless to control the forces of Nature, either in ourselves or in our physical environment, and keeps us in bondage to the same unthinking impulse by which the trees grow. Mind can liberate us from this bondage, by the power of impersonal thought, which enables us to judge critically the purely biological purposes towards which instinct more or less blindly tends. But mind, in its dealings with instinct, is *merely* critical: so far as instinct is concerned, the unchecked activity of the mind is apt to be destructive and to generate cynicism. Spirit is an antidote to the cynicism of mind: it universalizes the emotions that spring from instinct, and by universalizing them makes them impervious to mental criticism. And when thought is informed by spirit it loses its cruel, destructive quality; it no longer promotes the death of instinct, but only its purification from insistence and ruthlessness and its emancipation from the prison walls of accidental circumstance. It is instinct that gives force, mind that gives the means of directing force to desired ends, and spirit that suggests impersonal uses for force of a kind that thought cannot discredit by criticism. This is an outline of the parts that instinct, mind, and spirit would play in a harmonious life.

Instinct, mind, and spirit are each a help to the others when their development is free and unvitiated; but when corruption comes into any one of the three, not only does that one fail, but the others also become poisoned. All three must grow together. And if they are to grow to their full stature in any one man or woman, that man or woman must not be isolated, but must be one of a society where growth is not thwarted and made crooked.

The life of instinct, when it is unchecked by mind or spirit, consists of instinctive cycles, which begin with impulses to more or less definite acts, and pass on to satisfaction of needs through the consequences of these impulsive acts. Impulse and desire are not directed towards the whole cycle, but only towards its initiation: the rest is left to natural causes. We desire to eat, but we do not desire to be nourished unless we are valetudinarians. Yet without the nourishment eating is a mere momentary pleasure, not part of the general impulse to life. Men desire sexual intercourse, but they do not as a rule desire children strongly or often. Yet without the hope of children and its occasional realization, sexual intercourse remains for most people an isolated and separate pleasure, not uniting their personal life with the life of mankind, not continuous with the central purposes by which they live, and not capable of bringing that profound sense of fulfilment which comes from completion by children. Most men, unless the impulse is atrophied through disuse, feel a desire to create something, great or small according to their capacities. Some few are able to satisfy this desire: some happy men can create an Empire, a science, a poem, or a picture. The men of science, who have less difficulty than any others in finding an outlet for creativeness, are the happiest of intelligent men in the modern world, since their creative activity affords full satisfaction to mind and spirit as well as to the instinct of creation.[1] In them a beginning is to be seen of the new way of life which is to be sought; in their happiness we may perhaps find the germ of a future happiness for all mankind. The rest, with few exceptions, are thwarted in their creative impulses. They cannot build their own house or make their own garden, or direct their own labor to producing what their free choice would lead them to produce. In this way the instinct of creation, which should lead on to the life of mind and spirit, is checked and turned aside. Too often it is turned to destruction, as the only effective action which remains possible. Out of its defeat grows envy, and out of envy grows the impulse to destroy the creativeness of more fortunate men. This is one of the greatest sources of corruption in the life of instinct.

---

1    I should add artists but for the fact that most modern artists seem to find much greater difficulty in creation than men of science usually find.

The life of instinct is important, not only on its own account, or because of the direct usefulness of the actions which it inspires, but also because, if it is unsatisfactory, the individual life becomes detached and separated from the general life of man. All really profound sense of unity with others depends upon instinct, upon coöperation or agreement in some instinctive purpose. This is most obvious in the relations of men and women and parents and children. But it is true also in wider relations. It is true of large assemblies swayed by a strong common emotion, and even of a whole nation in times of stress. It is part of what makes the value of religion as a social institution. Where this feeling is wholly absent, other human beings seem distant and aloof. Where it is actively thwarted, other human beings become objects of instinctive hostility. The aloofness or the instinctive hostility may be masked by religious love, which can be given to all men regardless of their relation to ourselves. But religious love does not bridge the gulf that parts man from man: it looks across the gulf, it views others with compassion or impersonal sympathy, but it does not live with the same life with which they live. Instinct alone can do this, but only when it is fruitful and sane and direct. To this end it is necessary that instinctive cycles should be fairly often completed, not interrupted in the middle of their course. At present they are constantly interrupted, partly by purposes which conflict with them for economic or other reasons, partly by the pursuit of pleasure, which picks out the most agreeable part of the cycle and avoids the rest. In this way instinct is robbed of its importance and seriousness; it becomes incapable of bringing any real fulfilment, its demands grow more and more excessive, and life becomes no longer a whole with a single movement, but a series of detached moments, some of them pleasurable, most of them full of weariness and discouragement.

The life of the mind, although supremely excellent in itself, cannot bring health into the life of instinct, except when it results in a not too difficult outlet for the instinct of creation. In other cases it is, as a rule, too widely separated from instinct, too detached, too destitute of inward growth, to afford either a vehicle for instinct or a means of subtilizing and refining it. Thought is in its essence impersonal and detached, instinct is in its essence personal and tied to particular circumstances: between the two, unless both reach a high level, there is a war which is not easily appeased. This is the fundamental reason for vitalism, futurism, pragmatism, and the various other philosophies which advertise themselves as vigorous and virile. All these represent the attempt to find a mode of thought which shall not be hostile to instinct. The attempt, in itself, is deserving of praise, but the solution offered is far too facile. What is proposed amounts to a subordination of thought to instinct, a refusal to allow thought to achieve its own ideal. Thought which does not rise above what is personal is not thought in any true sense: it is merely a more or less intelligent use of instinct. It is thought and spirit that raise man above the level of the brutes. By discarding them we may lose the proper excellence of men, but cannot acquire the excellence of animals. Thought must achieve its full growth before a reconciliation with instinct is attempted.

When refined thought and unrefined instinct coexist, as they do in many intellectual men, the result is a complete disbelief in any important good to be achieved by the help of instinct. According to their disposition, some such men will as far as possible discard instinct and become ascetic, while others will accept it as a necessity, leaving it degraded and separated from all that is really important in their lives. Either of these courses prevents instinct from remaining vital, or from being a bond with others; either produces a sense of physical solitude, a gulf across which the minds and spirits of others may speak, but not their instincts. To very many men, the instinct of patriotism, when the war broke out, was the first instinct that had bridged the gulf, the first that had made them feel a really profound unity with others. This instinct, just because, in its intense form, it was new and unfamiliar, had remained uninfected by thought, not paralyzed or devitalized by doubt and cold detachment. The sense of unity which it brought is capable of being brought by the instinctive life of more normal times, if thought and spirit are not hostile to it. And so long as this sense of unity is absent, instinct and spirit cannot be in harmony, nor can the life of the community have vigor and the seeds of new growth.

The life of the mind, because of its detachment, tends to separate a man inwardly from other men, so long as it is not balanced by the life of the spirit. For this reason, mind without spirit can render instinct corrupt or atrophied, but cannot add any excellence to the life of instinct. On this ground, some men are hostile to thought. But no good purpose is served by trying to prevent the growth of thought, which has its own insistence, and if checked in the directions in which it tends naturally, will turn into other directions where it is more harmful. And thought is in itself god-like: if the opposition between thought and instinct were irreconcilable, it would be thought that ought to conquer. But the opposition is not irreconcilable: all that is necessary is that both thought and instinct should be informed by the life of the spirit.

In order that human life should have vigor, it is necessary for the instinctive impulses to be strong and direct; but in order that human life should be good, these impulses must be dominated and controlled by desires less personal and ruthless, less liable to lead to conflict than those that are inspired by instinct alone. Something impersonal and universal is needed over and above what springs out of the principle of individual growth. It is this that is given by the life of the spirit.

Patriotism affords an example of the kind of control which is needed. Patriotism is compounded out of a number of instinctive feelings and impulses: love of home, love of those whose ways and outlook resemble our own, the impulse to coöperation in a group, the sense of pride in the achievements of one's group. All these impulses and desires, like everything belonging to the life of instinct, are personal, in the sense that the feelings and actions which they inspire towards others are determined by the relation of those others to ourselves, not by what those others are intrinsically. All these impulses and desires unite to produce a love of man's own country which is more deeply implanted in the fiber of his being, and more closely united to his vital force, than any love not rooted in instinct. But if spirit does not enter in to generalize love of country, the exclusiveness of instinctive love makes it a source of hatred of other countries. What spirit can effect is to make us realize that other countries equally are worthy of love, that the vital warmth which makes us love our own country reveals to us that it deserves to be loved, and that only the poverty of our nature prevents us from loving all countries as we love our own. In this way instinctive love can be extended in imagination, and a sense of the value of all mankind can grow up, which is more living and intense than any that is possible to those whose instinctive love is weak. Mind can only show us that it is irrational to love our own country best; it can weaken patriotism, but cannot strengthen the love of all mankind. Spirit alone can do this, by extending and universalizing the love that is born of instinct. And in doing this it checks and purifies whatever is insistent or ruthless or oppressively personal in the life of instinct.

The same extension through spirit is necessary with other instinctive loves, if they are not to be enfeebled or corrupted by thought. The love of husband and wife is capable of being a very good thing, and when men and women are sufficiently primitive nothing but instinct and good fortune is needed to make it reach a certain limited perfection. But as thought begins to assert its right to criticize instinct the old simplicity becomes impossible. The love of husband and wife, as unchecked instinct leaves it, is too narrow and personal to stand against the shafts of satire, until it is enriched by the life of the spirit. The romantic view of marriage, which our fathers and mothers professed to believe, will not survive an imaginative peregrination down a street of suburban villas, each containing its couple, each couple having congratulated themselves as they first crossed the threshold, that here they could love in peace, without interruption from others, without contact with the cold outside world. The separateness and stuffiness, the fine names for cowardices and timid vanities, that are shut within the four walls of thousands upon thousands of little villas, present themselves coldly and mercilessly to those in whom mind is dominant at the expense of spirit.

Nothing is good in the life of a human being except the very best that his nature can achieve. As men advance, things which have been good cease to be good, merely because something better is possible. So it is with the life of instinct: for those whose mental life is strong, much that was really good while mind remained less developed has now become bad merely through the greater degree of truth in their outlook on the world. The instinctive man in love feels that his emotion is unique, that the lady of his heart has perfections such as no other woman ever equaled. The man who has acquired the power of impersonal thought realizes, when he is in love, that he is one of so many millions of men who are in love at this moment, that not more than one of all the millions can be right in thinking his love supreme, and that it is not likely that that one is oneself. He perceives that the state of being in love in those whose instinct is unaffected by thought or spirit, is a state of illusion, serving the ends of Nature and making a man a slave to the life of the species, not a willing minister to the impersonal ends which he sees to be good. Thought rejects this slavery; for no end that Nature may have in view will thought abdicate, or forgo its right to think truly. "Better the world should perish than that I or any other human being should believe a lie"—this is the religion of thought, in whose scorching flames the dross of the world is being burnt away. It is a good religion, and its work of destruction must be completed. But it is not all that man has need of. New growth must come after the destruction, and new growth can come only through the spirit.

Both patriotism and the love of man and woman, when they are merely instinctive, have the same defects: their exclusions, their enclosing walls, their indifference or hostility to the outside world. It is through this that thought is led to satire, that comedy has infected what men used to consider their holiest feelings. The satire and the comedy are justified, but not the death of instinct which they may produce if they remain in supreme command. They are justified, not as the last word of wisdom but as the gateway of pain through which men pass to a new life, where instinct is purified and yet nourished by the deeper desires and insight of spirit.

The man who has the life of the spirit within him views the love of man and woman, both in himself and in others, quite differently from the man who is exclusively dominated by mind. He sees, in his moments of insight, that in all human beings there is something deserving of love, something mysterious, something appealing, a cry out of the night, a groping journey, and a possible victory. When his instinct loves, he welcomes its help in seeing and feeling the value of the human being whom he loves. Instinct becomes a reinforcement to spiritual insight. What instinct tells him spiritual insight confirms, however much the mind may be aware of littlenesses, limitations, and enclosing walls that prevent the spirit from shining forth. His spirit divines in all men what his instinct shows him in the object of his love.

The love of parents for children has need of the same transformation. The purely instinctive love, unchecked by thought, uninformed by spirit, is exclusive, ruthless, and unjust. No benefit to others is felt, by the purely instinctive parent, to be worth an injury to one's own children. Honor and conventional morality place certain important practical limitations on the vicarious selfishness of parents, since a civilized community exacts a certain minimum before it will give respect. But within the limits allowed by public opinion, parental affection, when it is merely instinctive, will seek the advantage of children without regard to others. Mind can weaken the impulse to injustice, and diminish the force of instinctive love, but it cannot keep the whole force of instinctive love and turn it to more universal ends. Spirit can do this. It can leave the instinctive love of children undimmed, and extend the poignant devotion of a parent, in imagination, to the whole world. And parental love itself will prompt the parent who has the life of the spirit to give to his children the sense of justice, the readiness for service, the reverence, the will that controls self-seeking, which he feels to be a greater good than any personal success.

The life of the spirit has suffered in recent times by its association with traditional religion, by its apparent hostility to the life of the mind, and by the fact that it has seemed to center in renunciation. The life of the spirit demands readiness for renunciation when the occasion arises, but is in its essence as positive and as capable of enriching individual existence as mind and instinct are. It brings with it the joy of vision, of the mystery and profundity of the world, of the contemplation of life, and above all the joy of universal love. It liberates those who have it from the prison-house of insistent personal passion and mundane cares. It gives freedom and breadth and beauty to men's thoughts and feelings, and to all their relations with others. It brings the solution of doubts, the end of the feeling that all is vanity. It restores harmony between mind and instinct, and leads the separated unit back into his place in the life of mankind. For those who have once entered the world of thought, it is only through spirit that happiness and peace can return.

# VIII

## WHAT WE CAN DO

WHAT CAN WE do for the world while we live?
    Many men and women would wish to serve mankind, but they are perplexed and their power seems infinitesimal. Despair seizes them; those who have the strongest passion suffer most from the sense of impotence, and are most liable to spiritual ruin through lack of hope.

So long as we think only of the immediate future, it seems that what we can do is not much. It is probably impossible for us to bring the war to an end. We cannot destroy the excessive power of the State or of private property. We cannot, here and now, bring new life into education. In such matters, though we may see the evil, we cannot quickly cure it by any of the ordinary methods of politics. We must recognize that the world is ruled in a wrong spirit, and that a change of spirit will not come from one day to the next. Our expectations must not be for to-morrow, but for the time when what is thought now by a few shall have become the common thought of many. If we have courage and patience, we can think the thoughts and feel the hopes by which, sooner or later, men will be inspired, and weariness and discouragement will be turned into energy and ardor. For this reason, the first thing we have to do is to be clear in our own minds as to the kind of life we think good and the kind of change that we desire in the world.

The ultimate power of those whose thought is vital is far greater than it seems to men who suffer from the irrationality of contemporary politics. Religious toleration was once the solitary speculation of a few bold philosophers. Democracy, as a theory, arose among a handful of men in Cromwell's army; by them, after the Restoration, it was carried to America, where it came to fruition in the War of Independence. From America, Lafayette and the other Frenchmen who fought by the side of Washington brought the theory of democracy to France, where it united itself with the teaching of Rousseau and inspired the Revolution. Socialism, whatever we may think of its merits, is a great and growing power, which is transforming economic and political life; and socialism owes its origin to a very small number of isolated theorists. The movement against the subjection of women, which has become irresistible and is not far from complete triumph, began in the same way with a few impracticable idealists—Mary Wollstonecraft, Shelley, John Stuart Mill. The power of thought, in the long run, is greater than any other human power. Those who have the ability to think and the imagination to think in accordance with men's needs, are likely to achieve the good they aim at sooner or later, though probably not while they are still alive.

But those who wish to gain the world by thought must be content to lose it as a support in the present. Most men go through life without much questioning, accepting the beliefs and practices which they find current, feeling that the world will be their ally if they do not put themselves in opposition to it. New thought about the world is incompatible with this comfortable acquiescence; it requires a certain intellectual detachment, a certain solitary energy, a power of inwardly dominating the world and the outlook that the world engenders. Without some willingness to be lonely new thought cannot be achieved. And it will not be achieved to any purpose if the loneliness is accompanied by aloofness, so that the wish for union with others dies, or if intellectual detachment leads to contempt. It is because the state of mind required is subtle and difficult, because it is hard to be intellectually detached yet not aloof, that fruitful thought on human affairs is not common, and that most theorists are either conventional or sterile. The right kind of thought is rare and difficult, but it is not impotent. It is not the fear of impotence that need turn us aside from thought if we have the wish to bring new hope into the world.

In seeking a political theory which is to be useful at any given moment, what is wanted is not the invention of a Utopia, but the discovery of the best direction of movement. The direction which is good at one time may be superficially very different from that which is good at another time. Useful thought is that which indicates the right direction for the present time. But in judging what is the right direction there are two general principles which are always applicable.

1. The growth and vitality of individuals and communities is to be promoted as far as possible.

2. The growth of one individual or one community is to be as little as possible at the expense of another.

The second of these principles, as applied by an individual in his dealings with others, is the principle of *reverence*, that the life of another has the same importance which we feel in our own life. As applied impersonally in politics, it is the principle of *liberty*, or rather it includes the principle of liberty as a part. Liberty in itself is a negative principle; it tells us not to interfere, but does not give any basis for construction. It shows that many political and social institutions are bad and ought to be swept away, but it does not show what ought to be put in their place. For this reason a further principle is required, if our political theory is not to be purely destructive.

The combination of our two principles is not in practice an easy matter. Much of the vital energy of the world runs into channels which are oppressive. The Germans have shown themselves extraordinarily full of vital energy, but unfortunately in a form which seems incompatible with the vitality of their neighbors. Europe in general has more vital energy than Africa, but it has used its energy to drain Africa, through industrialism, of even such life as the negroes possessed. The vitality of southeastern Europe is being drained to supply cheap labor for the enterprise of American millionaires. The vitality of men has been in the past a hindrance to the development of women, and it is possible that in the near future women may become a similar hindrance to men. For such reasons the principle of reverence, though not in itself sufficient, is of very great importance, and is able to indicate many of the political changes that the world requires.

In order that both principles may be capable of being satisfied, what is needed is a unifying or integration, first of our individual lives, then of the life of the community and of the world, without sacrifice of individuality. The life of an individual, the life of a community, and even the life of mankind, ought to be, not a number of separate fragments but in some sense a whole. When this is the case, the growth of the individual is fostered, and is not incompatible with the growth of other individuals. In this way the two principles are brought into harmony.

What integrates an individual life is a consistent creative purpose or unconscious direction. Instinct alone will not suffice to give unity to the life of a civilized man or woman: there must be some dominant object, an ambition, a desire for scientific or artistic creation, a religious principle, or strong and lasting affections. Unity of life is very difficult for a man or woman who has suffered a certain kind of defeat, the kind by which what should have been the dominant impulse is checked and made abortive. Most professions inflict this kind of defeat upon a man at the very outset. If a man becomes a journalist, he probably has to write for a newspaper whose politics he dislikes; this kills his pride in work and his sense of independence. Most medical men find it very hard to succeed without humbug, by which whatever scientific conscience they may have had is destroyed. Politicians are obliged, not only to swallow the party program but to pretend to be saints, in order to conciliate religious supporters; hardly any man can enter Parliament without hypocrisy. In no profession is there any respect for the native pride without which a man cannot remain whole; the world ruthlessly crushes it out, because it implies independence, and men desire to enslave others more than they desire to be free themselves. Inward freedom is infinitely precious, and a society which will preserve it is immeasurably to be desired.

The principle of growth in a man is not crushed necessarily by preventing him from doing some definite thing, but it is often crushed by persuading him to do something else. The things that crush growth are those that produce a sense of impotence in the directions in which the vital impulse wishes to be effective. The worst things are those to which the will assents. Often, chiefly from failure of self-knowledge, a man's will is on a lower level than his impulse: his impulse is towards some kind of creation, while his will is towards a conventional career, with a sufficient income and the respect of his contemporaries. The stereotyped illustration is the artist who produces shoddy work to please the public. But something of the artist's definiteness of impulse exists in very many men who are not artists. Because the impulse is deep and dumb, because what is called common sense is often against it, because a young man can only follow it if he is willing to set up his own obscure feelings against the wisdom and prudent maxims of elders and friends, it happens in ninety-nine cases out of a hundred that the creative impulse, out of which a free and vigorous life might have sprung, is checked and thwarted at the very outset: the young man consents to become a tool, not an independent workman; a mere means to the fulfilment of others, not the artificer of what his own nature feels to be good. In the moment when he makes this act of consent something dies within him. He can never again become a whole man, never again have the undamaged self-respect, the upright pride, which might have kept him happy in his soul in spite of all outward troubles and difficulties—except, indeed, through conversion and a fundamental change in his way of life.

Outward prohibitions, to which the will gives no assent, are far less harmful than the subtler inducements which seduce the will. A serious disappointment in love may cause the most poignant pain, but to a vigorous man it will not do the same inward damage as is done by marrying for money. The achievement of this or that special desire is not what is essential: what is essential is the direction, the *kind* of effectiveness which is sought. When the fundamental impulse is opposed by will, it is made to feel helpless: it has no longer enough hope to be powerful as a motive. Outward compulsion does not do the same damage unless it produces the same sense of impotence; and it will not produce the same sense of impotence if the impulse is strong and courageous. Some thwarting of special desires is unavoidable even in the best imaginable community, since some men's desires, unchecked, lead to the oppression or destruction of others. In a good community Napoleon could not have been allowed the profession of his choice, but he might have found happiness as a pioneer in Western America. He could not have found happiness as a City clerk, and no tolerable organization of society would compel him to become a City clerk.

The integration of an individual life requires that it should embody whatever creative impulse a man may possess, and that his education should have been such as to elicit and fortify this impulse. The integration of a community requires that the different creative impulses of different men and women should work together towards some common life, some common purpose, not necessarily conscious, in which all the members of the community find a help to their individual fulfilment. Most of the activities that spring from vital impulses consist of two parts: one creative, which furthers one's own life and that of others with the same kind of impulse or circumstances, and one possessive, which hinders the life of some group with a different kind of impulse or circumstances. For this reason, much of what is in itself most vital may nevertheless work against life, as, for example, seventeenth-century Puritanism did in England, or as nationalism does throughout Europe at the present day. Vitality easily leads to strife or oppression, and so to loss of vitality. War, at its outset, integrates the life of a nation, but it disintegrates the life of the world, and in the long run the life of a nation too, when it is as severe as the present war.

The war has made it clear that it is impossible to produce a secure integration of the life of a single community while the relations between civilized countries are governed by aggressiveness and suspicion. For this reason any really powerful movement of reform will have to be international. A merely national movement is sure to fail through fear of danger from without. Those who desire a better world, or even a radical improvement in their own country, will have to coöperate with those who have similar desires in other countries, and to devote much of their energy to overcoming that blind hostility which the war has intensified. It is not in partial integrations, such as patriotism alone can produce, that any ultimate hope is to be found. The problem is, in national and international questions as in the individual life, to keep what is creative in vital impulses, and at the same time to turn into other channels the part which is at present destructive.

Men's impulses and desires may be divided into those that are creative and those that are possessive. Some of our activities are directed to creating what would not otherwise exist, others are directed towards acquiring or retaining what exists already. The typical creative impulse is that of the artist; the typical possessive impulse is that of property. The best life is that in which creative impulses play the largest part and possessive impulses the smallest. The best institutions are those which produce the greatest possible creativeness and the least possessiveness compatible with self-preservation. Possessiveness may be defensive or aggressive: in the criminal law it is defensive, and in criminals it is aggressive. It may perhaps be admitted that the criminal law is less abominable than the criminal, and that defensive possessiveness is unavoidable so long as aggressive possessiveness exists. But not even the most purely defensive forms of possessiveness are in themselves admirable; indeed, as soon as they are strong they become hostile to the creative impulses. "Take no thought, saying, What shall we eat? or What shall we drink, or Wherewithal shall we be clothed?" Whoever has known a strong creative impulse has known the value of this precept in its exact and literal sense: it is preoccupation with possessions, more than anything else, that prevents men from living freely and nobly. The State and Property are the great embodiments of possessiveness; it is for this reason that they are against life, and that they issue in war. Possession means taking or keeping some good thing which another is prevented from enjoying; creation means putting into the world a good thing which otherwise no one would be able to enjoy. Since the material goods of the world must be divided among the population, and since some men are by nature brigands, there must be defensive possession, which will be regulated, in a good community, by some principle of impersonal justice. But all this is only the preface to a good life or good political institutions, in which creation will altogether outweigh possession, and distributive justice will exist as an uninteresting matter of course.

The supreme principle, both in politics and in private life, should be *to promote all that is creative, and so to diminish the impulses and desires that center round possession.* The State at present is very largely an embodiment of possessive impulses: internally, it protects the rich against the poor; externally, it uses force for the exploitation of inferior races, and for competition with other States. Our whole economic system is concerned exclusively with possession; yet the production of goods is a form of creation, and except in so far as it is irredeemably mechanical and monotonous, it might afford a vehicle for creative impulses. A great deal might be achieved towards this end by forming the producers of a certain kind of commodity into an autonomous democracy, subject to State control as regards the price of their commodity but not as to the manner of its production.

Education, marriage, and religion are essentially creative, yet all three have been vitiated by the intrusion of possessive motives. Education is usually treated as a means of prolonging the *status quo* by instilling prejudices, rather than of creating free thought and a noble outlook by the example of generous feeling and the stimulus of mental adventure. In marriage, love, which is creative, is kept in chains by jealousy, which is possessive. Religion, which should set free the creative vision of the spirit, is usually more concerned to repress the life of instinct and to combat the subversiveness of thought. In all these ways the fear that grows out of precarious possession has replaced the hope inspired by creative force. The wish to plunder others is recognized, in theory, to be bad; but the fear of being plundered is little better. Yet these two motives between them dominate nine-tenths of politics and private life.

The creative impulses in different men are essentially harmonious, since what one man creates cannot be a hindrance to what another is wishing to create. It is the possessive impulses that involve conflict. Although, morally and politically, the creative and possessive impulses are opposites, yet psychologically either passes easily into the other, according to the accidents of circumstance and opportunity. The genesis of impulses and the causes which make them change ought to be studied; education and social institutions ought to be made such as to strengthen the impulses which harmonize in different men, and to weaken those that involve conflict. I have no doubt that what might be accomplished in this way is almost unlimited.

It is rather through impulse than through will that individual lives and the life of the community can derive the strength unity of a single direction. Will is of two kinds, of which one is directed outward and the other inward. The first, which is directed outward, is called into play by external obstacles, either the opposition of others or the technical difficulties of an undertaking. This kind of will is an expression of strong impulse or desire, whenever instant success is impossible; it exists in all whose life is vigorous, and only decays when their vital force is enfeebled. It is necessary to success in any difficult enterprise, and without it great achievement is very rare. But the will which is directed inward is only necessary in so far as there is an inner conflict of impulses or desires; a perfectly harmonious nature would have no occasion for inward will. Such perfect harmony is of course a scarcely realizable ideal: in all men impulses arise which are incompatible with their central purpose, and which must be checked if their life as a whole is not to be a failure. But this will happen least with those whose central impulses are strongest; and it will happen less often in a society which aims at freedom than in a society like ours, which is full of artificial incompatibilities created by antiquated institutions and a tyrannous public opinion. The power to exert inward will when the occasion arises must always be needed by those who wish their lives to embody some central purpose, but with better institutions the occasions when inward will is necessary might be made fewer and less important. This result is very much to be desired, because when will checks impulses which are only accidentally harmful, it diverts a force which might be spent on overcoming outward obstacles, and if the impulses checked are strong and serious, it actually diminishes the vital force available. A life full of inhibitions is likely not to remain a very vigorous life but to become listless and without zest. Impulse tends to die when it is constantly held in check, and if it does not die, it is apt to work underground, and issue in some form much worse than that in which it has been checked. For these reasons the necessity for using inward will ought to be avoided as much as possible, and consistency of action ought to spring rather from consistency of impulse than from control of impulse by will.

The unifying of life ought not to demand the suppression of the casual desires that make amusement and play; on the contrary, everything ought to be done to make it easy to combine the main purposes of life with all kinds of pleasure that are not in their nature harmful. Such things as habitual drunkenness, drugs, cruel sports, or pleasure in inflicting pain are essentially harmful, but most of the amusements that civilized men naturally enjoy are either not harmful at all or only accidentally harmful through some effect which might be avoided in a better society. What is needed is, not asceticism or a drab Puritanism, but capacity for strong impulses and desires directed towards large creative ends. When such impulses and desires are vigorous, they bring with them, of themselves, what is needed to make a good life.

But although amusement and adventure ought to have their share, it is impossible to create a good life if they are what is mainly desired. Subjectivism, the habit of directing thought and desire to our own states of mind rather than to something objective, inevitably makes life fragmentary and unprogressive. The man to whom amusement is the end of life tends to lose interest gradually in the things out of which he has been in the habit of obtaining amusement, since he does not value these things on their own account, but on account of the feelings which they arouse in him. When they are no longer amusing, boredom drives him to seek some new stimulus, which fails him in its turn. Amusement consists in a series of moments without any essential continuity; a purpose which unifies life is one which requires some prolonged activity, and is like building a monument rather than a child's castle in the sand.

Subjectivism has other forms beside the mere pursuit of amusement. Many men, when they are in love, are more interested in their own emotion than in the object of their love; such love does not lead to any essential union, but leaves fundamental separateness undiminished. As soon as the emotion grows less vivid the experience has served its purpose, and there seems no motive for prolonging it. In another way, the same evil of subjectivism was fostered by Protestant religion and morality, since they directed attention to sin and the state of the soul rather than to the outer world and our relations with it. None of these forms of subjectivism can prevent a man's life from being fragmentary and isolated. Only a life which springs out of dominant impulses directed to objective ends can be a satisfactory whole, or be intimately united with the lives of others.

The pursuit of pleasure and the pursuit of virtue alike suffer from subjectivism: Epicureanism and Stoicism are infected with the same taint. Marcus Aurelius, enacting good laws in order that he might be virtuous, is not an attractive figure. Subjectivism is a natural outcome of a life in which there is much more thought than action: while outer things are being remembered or desired, not actually experienced, they seem to become mere ideas. What they are in themselves becomes less interesting to us than the effects which they produce in our own minds. Such a result tends to be brought about by increasing civilization, because increasing civilization continually diminishes the need for vivid action and enhances the opportunities for thought. But thought will not have this bad result if it is active thought, directed towards achieving some purpose; it is only passive thought that leads to subjectivism. What is needed is to keep thought in intimate union with impulses and desires, making it always itself an activity with an objective purpose. Otherwise, thought and impulse become enemies, to the great detriment of both.

In order to make the lives of average men and women less fragmentary and separate, and to give greater opportunity for carrying out creative impulses, it is not enough to know the goal we wish to reach, or to proclaim the excellence of what we desire to achieve. It is necessary to understand the effect of institutions and beliefs upon the life of impulse, and to discover ways of improving this effect by a change in institutions. And when this intellectual work has been done, our thought will still remain barren unless we can bring it into relation with some powerful political force. The only powerful political force from which any help is to be expected in bringing about such changes as seem needed is Labor. The changes required are very largely such as Labor may be expected to welcome, especially during the time of hardship after the war. When the war is over, labor discontent is sure to be very prevalent throughout Europe, and to constitute a political force by means of which a great and sweeping reconstruction may be effected.

The civilized world has need of fundamental change if it is to be saved from decay—change both in its economic structure and in its philosophy of life. Those of us who feel the need of change must not sit still in dull despair: we can, if we choose, profoundly influence the future. We can discover and preach the kind of change that is required—the kind that preserves what is positive in the vital beliefs of our time, and, by eliminating what is negative and inessential, produces a synthesis to which all that is not purely reactionary can give allegiance. As soon as it has become clear what *kind* of change is required, it will be possible to work out its parts in more detail. But until the war is ended there is little use in detail, since we do not know what kind of world the war will leave. The only thing that seems indubitable is that much new thought will be required in the new world produced by the war. Traditional views will give little help. It is clear that men's most important actions are not guided by the sort of motives that are emphasized in traditional political philosophies. The impulses by which the war has been produced and sustained come out of a deeper region than that of most political argument. And the opposition to the war on the part of those few who have opposed it comes from the same deep region. A political theory, if it is to hold in times of stress, must take account of the impulses that underlie explicit thought: it must appeal to them, and it must discover how to make them fruitful rather than destructive.

Economic systems have a great influence in promoting or destroying life. Except slavery, the present industrial system is the most destructive of life that has ever existed. Machinery and large-scale production are ineradicable, and must survive in any better system which is to replace the one under which we live. Industrial federal democracy is probably the best direction for reform to take.

Philosophies of life, when they are widely believed, also have a very great influence on the vitality of a community. The most widely accepted philosophy of life at present is that what matters most to a man's happiness is his income. This philosophy, apart from other demerits, is harmful because it leads men to aim at a result rather than an activity, an enjoyment of material goods in which men are not differentiated, rather than a creative impulse which embodies each man's individuality. More refined philosophies, such as are instilled by higher education, are too apt to fix attention on the past rather than the future, and on correct behavior rather than effective action. It is not in such philosophies that men will find the energy to bear lightly the weight of tradition and of ever-accumulating knowledge.

The world has need of a philosophy, or a religion, which will promote life. But in order to promote life it is necessary to value something other than mere life. Life devoted only to life is animal without any real human value, incapable of preserving men permanently from weariness and the feeling that all is vanity. If life is to be fully human it must serve some end which seems, in some sense, outside human life, some end which is impersonal and above mankind, such as God or truth or beauty. Those who best promote life do not have life for their purpose. They aim rather at what seems like a gradual incarnation, a bringing into our human existence of something eternal, something that appears to imagination to live in a heaven remote from strife and failure and the devouring jaws of Time. Contact with this eternal world—even if it be only a world of our imagining—brings a strength and a fundamental peace which cannot be wholly destroyed by the struggles and apparent failures of our temporal life. It is this happy contemplation of what is eternal that Spinoza calls the intellectual love of God. To those who have once known it, it is the key of wisdom.

What we have to do practically is different for each one of us, according to our capacities and opportunities. But if we have the life of the spirit within us, what we must do and what we must avoid will become apparent to us.

By contact with what is eternal, by devoting our life to bringing something of the Divine into this troubled world, we can make our own lives creative even now, even in the midst of the cruelty and strife and hatred that surround us on every hand. To make the individual life creative is far harder in a community based on possession than it would be in such a community as human effort may be able to build up in the future. Those who are to begin the regeneration of the world must face loneliness, opposition, poverty, obloquy. They must be able to live by truth and love, with a rational unconquerable hope; they must be honest and wise, fearless, and guided by a consistent purpose. A body of men and women so inspired will conquer—first the difficulties and perplexities of their individual lives, then, in time, though perhaps only in a long time, the outer world. Wisdom and hope are what the world needs; and though it fights against them, it gives its respect to them in the end.

When the Goths sacked Rome, St. Augustine wrote the "City of God," putting a spiritual hope in place of the material reality that had been destroyed. Throughout the centuries that followed St. Augustine's hope lived and gave life, while Rome sank to a village of hovels. For us, too, it is necessary to create a new hope, to build up by our thought a better world than the one which is hurling itself into ruin. Because the times are bad, more is required of us than would be required in normal times. Only a supreme fire of thought and spirit can save future generations from the death that has befallen the generation which we knew and loved.

It has been my good fortune to come in contact as a teacher with young men of many different nations—young men in whom hope was alive, in whom the creative energy existed that would have realized in the world some part at least of the imagined beauty by which they lived. They have been swept into the war, some on one side, some on the other. Some are still fighting, some are maimed for life, some are dead; of those who survive it is to be feared that many will have lost the life of the spirit, that hope will have died, that energy will be spent, and that the years to come will be only a weary journey towards the grave. Of all this tragedy, not a few of those who teach seem to have no feeling: with ruthless logic, they prove that these young men have been sacrificed unavoidably for some coldly abstract end; undisturbed themselves, they lapse quickly into comfort after any momentary assault of feeling. In such men the life of the spirit is dead. If it were living, it would go out to meet the spirit in the young, with a love as poignant as the love of father or mother. It would be unaware of the bounds of self; their tragedy would be its own. Something would cry out: "No, this is not right; this is not good; this is not a holy cause, in which the brightness of youth is destroyed and dimmed. It is we, the old, who have sinned; we have sent these young men to the battlefield for our evil passions, our spiritual death, our failure to live generously out of the warmth of the heart and out of the living vision of the spirit. Let us come out of this death, for it is we who are dead, not the young men who have died through our fear of life. Their very ghosts have more life than we: they hold us up for ever to the shame and obloquy of all the ages to come. Out of their ghosts must come life, and it is we whom they must vivify."

# THE ETHICS OF WAR

THE QUESTION WHETHER war is ever justified, and if so under what circumstances, is one which has been forcing itself upon the attention of all thoughtful men. On this question I find myself in the somewhat painful position of holding that no single one of the combatants is justified in the present war, while not taking the extreme Tolstoyan view that war is under all circumstances a crime. Opinions on such a subject as war are the outcome of feeling rather than of thought: given a man's emotional temperament, his convictions, both on war in general, and on any particular war which may occur during his lifetime, can be predicted with tolerable certainty. The arguments used will be mere reinforcements to convictions otherwise reached. The fundamental facts in this as in all ethical questions are feelings; all that thought can do is to clarify and systematize the expression of those feelings, and it is such clarifying and systematizing of my own feelings that I wish to attempt in the present article.

## I.

The question of the rights and wrongs of a particular war is generally considered from a juridical or quasi-juridical standpoint: so and so broke such and such a treaty, crossed such and such a frontier, committed such and such technically unfriendly acts, and therefore by the rules it is permissible to kill as many of his nation as modern armaments render possible. There is a certain unreality, a certain lack of imaginative grasp about this way of viewing matters. It has the advantage, always dearly prized by lazy men, of substituting a formula, at once ambiguous and easily applied, for the vital realization of the consequences of acts. The juridical point of view is in fact an illegitimate transference, to the relations of States, of principles properly applicable to the relation of individuals within a State. Within a State, private war is forbidden, and the disputes of private citizens are settled, not by their own force, but by the force of the police, which, being overwhelming, very seldom needs to be explicitly displayed. It is necessary that there should be rules according to which the police decide who is to be considered in the right in a private dispute. These rules constitute law. The chief gain derived from the law and the police is the abolition of private wars, and this gain is independent of the question whether the law as it stands is the best possible. It is therefore in the public interest that the man who goes against the law should be considered in the wrong, not because of the excellence of the law, but because of the importance of avoiding the resort to force as between individuals within the State.

In the interrelation of States nothing of the same sort exists. There is, it is true, a body of conventions called "international law," and there are innumerable treaties between High Contracting Powers. But the conventions and the treaties differ from anything that could properly be called law by the absence of sanction: there is no police force able or willing to enforce their observance. It follows from this that every nation concludes multitudes of divergent and incompatible treaties, and that, in spite of the high language one sometimes hears, the main purpose of the treaties is in actual fact to afford the sort of pretext which is considered respectable for engaging in war with another Power. A Power is considered unscrupulous when it goes to war without previously providing itself with such a pretext – unless indeed its opponent is a small country, in which case it is only to be blamed if that small country happens to be under the protection of some other Great Power. England and Russia may partition Persia immediately after guaranteeing its integrity an independence, because no other Great Power has a recognized interest in Persia, and Persia is one of those small States in regard to which treaty obligations are not considered binding. France and Spain, under a similar guarantee as to Morocco, must not partition it without first compensating Germany, because it is recognized that, until such compensation has been offered and accepted, Germany, though not Morocco, has a legitimate interest in the preservation of that country. All Great Powers having guaranteed the neutrality of Belgium, England has a recognized right to resent its violation – a right which is exercised when it is believed to be to England's interest, and waived when England's interest is not thought to be involved. A treaty is therefore not to be regarded as a contract having the same kind of binding force as belongs to private contracts; it is to be regarded merely as a means of giving notice to rival powers that certain acts may, if the national interest so demand, form one of those reasons for war which are recognized as legitimate.

If the faithful observance of treaties were a frequent occurrence, like the observance of contracts, the breach of a treaty might be a real and not merely a formal ground for war, since it would tend to weaken the practice of deciding disputes by agreement rather than by armed force. In the absence of such a practice, however, appeal to treaties is only to be regarded as part of the diplomatic machinery. A nation whose diplomacy has been skilfully conducted will always, when it belies that its interests demand war, be able to find some treaty or agreement bringing its intervention within the rules of the diplomatic game. It is obvious, however, that, so long as treaties are only observed when it is convenient to do so, the rules of the diplomatic game have nothing to do with the question whether embarking or participating in a war will or will not be for the good of mankind, and it is this question which has to be decided in considering whether a war is justified or not.

## II.

It is necessary, in regard to any war, to consider, not its paper justification in past agreements, but its real justification in the balance of good which it is to bring to mankind. At the beginning of a war each nation, under the influence of what is called patriotism, believes that its own victory is both certain and of great importance to mankind. The praiseworthiness of this belief has become an accepted maxim of common sense: even when war is actually in progress it is held to be natural and right that a citizen of an enemy country should regard the victory of his side as assured and highly desirable. By concentrating attention upon the supposed advantages of the victory of our own side, we become more or less blind to the evils inseparable from war and equally certain whichever side may ultimately prove victorious. Yet so long as these are not fully realized, it is impossible to judge justly whether a war is or is not likely to be beneficial to the human race. Although the theme is trite, it is necessary therefore briefly to remind ourselves what the evils of war really are.

To begin with the most obvious evil: large numbers of young men, the most courageous and the most physically fit in their respective nations, are killed, bringing great sorrow to their friends, loss to the community, and gain only to themselves. Many others are maimed for life, some go mad, and others become nervous wrecks, mere useless and helpless derelicts. Of those who survive many will be brutalized and morally degraded by the fierce business of killing, which, however much it may be the soldier's duty, must shock and often destroy the more humane instincts. As every truthful record of war shows, fear and hate let loose the wild beast in a not inconsiderable proportion of combatants, leading to strange cruelties, which must be faced, but not dwelt upon if sanity is to be preserved.

Of the evils of war to the non-combatant population in the regions where fighting occurs, the recent misfortunes of Belgium have afforded an example upon which it is not necessary to enlarge. It is necessary, however, to point out that the misfortunes of Belgium do not, as is commonly believed in England, afford a reason in favor of war. Hatred, by a tragic delusion, perpetuates the very evils from which it springs. The sufferings of Belgium are attributed to the Germans and not to war; and thus the very horrors of the war are used to stimulate the desire to increase their area and intensity. Even assuming the utmost humanity compatible with the conduct of military operations, it cannot be doubted that, if the troops of the Allies penetrate into the industrial regions of Germany, the German population will have to suffer a great part of the misfortunes which Germany has inflicted upon Belgium. To men under the influence of hate this thought is a cause of rejoicing, but to men in whom humane feeling is not extinct it shows that our sympathy with Belgium should make us hate war rather than Germany.

The evils which war produces outside the area of military operations are perhaps even more serious, for though less intense they are far more widespread. Passing by the anxiety and sorrow of those whose sons or husbands or brothers are at the front, the extent and consequences of the economic injury inflicted by war are much greater than is usually realized. It is common to speak of economic evils as merely material, and of desire for economic progress as groveling and uninspired. This view is perhaps natural in well-to-do people, to whom economic progress means setting up a motor car or taking holidays in Scotland instead of at the seaside. But with regard to the poorer classes of society, economic progress is the first condition of many spiritual goods and even often of life itself. An overcrowded family, living in a slum in conditions of filth and immorality, where half the children die from ignorance of hygiene and bad sanitation, and the remainder grow up stunted and ignorant-such a family can hardly make progress mentally or spiritually, except through an improvement in its economic condition. And without going to the very bottom of the social scale, economic progress is essential to the possibility of good education, of a tolerable existence for women, and of that breadth and freedom of outlook upon which any solid and national advance must be based. It is not the most oppressed or the most ill-used who make an effective plea for social justice, for some reorganization of society which shall give less to the idler and more to the common man. Throughout the Napoleonic wars, while the landowners of England continually increased their rent-rolls, the mass of the wage-earning population sank into greater and greater destitution. It was only afterwards, during the long peace, that a less unjust distribution began to be possible. It cannot be doubted that the desire on the part of the rich to distract men's minds from the claims of social justice has been more or less unconsciously one of the motives leading to war in modern Europe. Everywhere the well-to-do and the political parties which represent their interests have been the chief agents in stirring up international hatred and in persuading the working man that his real enemy is the foreigner. Thus war, and the fear of war, has a double-effect in retarding social progress: it diminishes the resources available for improving the condition of the wage-earning classes, and it distracts men's minds from the need and possibility of general improvement by persuading them that the way to better themselves is to injure their comrades in some other country. It is as a protest against this delusion that international socialism has arisen, and whatever may be thought of socialism as an economic doctrine, its internationalism makes it the sanest force in modern politics, and the only body which has preserved some degree of judgment and humanity in the present chaos.

Of all the evils of war the greatest, in my opinion, is the purely spiritual evil: the hatred, the injustice, the repudiation of truth, the artificial conflict, where, if once the blindness of atavistic instincts and the sinister influence of anti-social interests, such as those of armaments with their subservient press, could be overcome, it would be seen that there is a real consonance of interest and essential identity of human nature, and every reason to replace hatred by love. Mr. Norman Angell has well shown how unreal, as applied to the conflicts of civilized States, is the whole vocabulary of international conflict, how illusory are the gains supposed to be obtained by victory, and how fallacious are the injuries which nations, in times of peace, are supposed to inflict upon each other in economic competition. The importance of this thesis lies, not so much in its direct economic application, as in the hope which it affords for the liberation of better spiritual impulses in the relations of different communities. To love our enemies, however desirable, is not easy; and therefore it is well to realize that the enmity springs only from blindness, not from any inexorable physical necessity.

## III.

Are there any wars which achieve so much for the good of mankind as to outweigh all the evils we have been considering? I think there have been such wars in the past, but they are not wars of the sort with which our diplomatists are concerned, for which our armies and navies have been prepared, and which are exemplified by the present conflict. For purposes of classification we may roughly distinguish four kinds of wars, though of course in any given case a war is not likely to be quite clearly of any one of the four kinds. With this proviso we may distinguish: (1) Wars of Colonization; (2) Wars of Principle; (3) Wars of Self-defence; (4) Wars of Prestige. Of these four kinds I should say that the first and second are fairly often justified; the third seldom, except against an adversary of inferior civilization; and the fourth, which is the sort to which the present war belongs, never. Let us consider these four kinds of war in succession.

By a "war of colonization" I mean a war whose purpose is to drive out the whole population of some territory and replace it by an invading population of a different race. Ancient wars were very largely of this kind, of which we have a good example in the Book of Joshua. In modern times the conflicts of Europeans with American-Indians, Maoris, and other aborigines in temperate regions, have been of this kind. Such wars are totally devoid of technical justification, and are apt to be more ruthless than any other war. Nevertheless, if we are to judge by results, we cannot regret that such wars have taken place. They have the merit, often quite fallaciously claimed for all wars, of leading in the main to the survival of the fittest, and it is chiefly through such wars that the civilized portion of the world has been extended from the neighborhood of the Mediterranean to the greater part of the earth's surface. The eighteenth century, which liked to praise the virtues of the savage and contrast them with the gilded corruption of courts, nevertheless had no scruple in thrusting the noble savage out from his North American hunting grounds. And we cannot at this date bring ourselves to condemn the process by which the American continent has been acquired for European civilization. In order that such wars may be justified, it is necessary that there should be a very great and undeniable difference between the civilization of the colonizers and that of the dispossessed natives. It is necessary also that the climate should be one in which the invading race can flourish. When these conditions are satisfied the conquest becomes justified, though actual fighting against the dispossessed inhabitants ought, of course, to be avoided as far as is compatible with colonizing. Many humane people will object in theory to the justification of this form of robbery, but I do not think that any practical or effective objection is likely to be made.

Such wars, however, belong now to the past. The regions where the white men can live are all allotted, either to white races or to yellow races to whom the white man is not clearly superior, and whom, in any case, he is not strong enough to expel. Apart from small punitive expeditions, wars of colonization, in the true sense, are no longer possible. What are nowadays called colonial wars do not aim at the complete occupation of a country by a conquering race; they aim only at securing certain governmental and trading advantages. They belong, in fact, rather with what I call wars of prestige, than with wars of colonization in the old sense. There are, it is true, a few rare exceptions. The Greeks in the second Balkan war conducted a war of colonization against the Bulgarians; throughout a certain territory which they intended to occupy, they killed all the men, and carried off all the women. But in such cases, the only possible justification fails, since there is no evidence of superior civilization on the side of the conquerors.

In spite, however, of the fact that wars of colonization belong to the past, men's feelings and beliefs about war are still those appropriate to the extinct conditions which rendered such wars possible. When the present war began, many people in England imagined that if the Allies were victorious Germany would cease to exist: Germany was to be "destroyed" or "smashed," and since these phrases sounded vigorous and cheering, people failed to see that they were totally devoid of meaning. There are some seventy million Germans; with great good fortune, we might, in a successful war, succeed in killing two millions of them. There would then still be sixty-eight million Germans, and in a few years the loss of population due to the war would be made good. Germany is not merely a State, but a nation, bound together by a common language, common traditions, and common ideals. Whatever the outcome of the war, this nation will still exist at the end of it, and its strength cannot be permanently impaired. But imagination in what pertains to war is still dominated by Homer and the Old Testament; men who cannot see that circumstances have changed since those works were composed are called "practical" men and are said to be free

from illusions. Those, on the other hand, who have some understanding of the modern world, and some capacity for freeing their minds
from the influence of phrases, are called dreamy idealists, Utopians,,
traitors, and friends of every country but their own. If the facts were
understood, wars amongst civilized nations would cease, owing to
their inherent absurdity. Men's passions always lag behind their political organizations, and facts which leave no outlet for passions are not
readily admitted. In order that hatred, pride and violence may find
an outlet, men unconsciously blind themselves to the plainest facts of
politics and economics, and modern war continues to be waged with
the phrases and theories invented by simpler men in a simpler age.

## IV.

The second type of war which may sometimes be justified is what
may be called "the war of principle." To this kind belong the wars of
Protestant and Catholic, and the English and American civil wars. In
such cases, each side, or at least one side, is honestly convinced that
the progress of mankind depends upon the adoption of certain beliefs
– beliefs which, through blindness or natural depravity, mankind will
not regard as reasonable, except when presented at the point of the
bayonet. Such wars may be justified: for example, a nation practising
religious toleration may be justified in resisting a persecuting nation
holding a different creed. On this ground we might justify the resistance of the Dutch to the English and French combined in the time of
Charles II. But wars of principle are much less often justified than is
believed by those in whose age they occur. It is very rarely that a principle of genuine value to mankind can only be propagated by military
force: as a rule, it is the bad part of men's principles, not the good part,
which makes it necessary to fight for their defence. And for this reason
the bad part rather than the good rises to prominence during the progress of the war of principle. A nation undertaking a war in defence of
religious toleration would be almost certain to persecute those of its
citizens who did not believe in religious toleration. A war on behalf of
democracy, if it is long and fierce, is sure to end in the exclusion from
all share of power of those who do not support the war.

Mr. George Trevelyan in an eloquent passage describes the defeat
which, as the ultimate outcome of our civil war, overtook alike the
ideals of the Roundheads and the ideals of the Cavaliers. "And this
was the curse of the victors, not to die, but to live, and almost to lose

their awful faith in God, when they saw the Restoration, not of the old gaiety that was too gay for them and the old loyalty that was too loyal for them, but of corruption and selfishness that had neither country nor king. The sound of the Roundhead cannon has long ago died away, but still the silence of the garden is heavy with unalterable fate, brooding over besiegers and besieged, in such haste to destroy each other and permit only the vile to survive."[1] This common doom of opposite ideals is the usual, though not the invariable, penalty of supporting ideals by force. While it may therefore be conceded that such wars are not invariably to be condemned, we must nevertheless scrutinize very skeptically the claim of any particular war to be justified on the ground of the victory which it brings to some important principle.

There are some who maintain that the present war is a war in defence of democracy. I do not know whether this view is adopted by the Tsar, and for the sake of the stability of the Alliance I sincerely hope that it is not. I do not, however, desire to dispute the proposition that democracy in the western nations would suffer from the victory of Germany. What I do wish to dispute is the belief not infrequently entertained in England that if the Allies are victorious democracy can be forced upon a reluctant Germany as part of the conditions of peace. Men who think thus have lost sight of the spirit of democracy in worship of the letter. The Germans have the form of government which they desire, and therefore any other form, imposed by alien victors, would be less in harmony with the spirit of democracy, however much it might conform to the letter. Men do right to desire strongly the victory of ideals which they believe to be important, but it is almost always a sign of yielding to undue impatience when men believe that what is valuable in their ideals can be furthered by the substitution of force for peaceful persuasion. To advocate democracy by war is only to repeat, on a vaster scale and with far more tragic results, the error of those who have sought it hitherto by the assassin's knife and the bomb of the anarchist.

## V.

The next kind of war to be considered is the war of self-defence. This kind of war is almost universally admitted to be justifiable, and is condemned only by Christ and Tolstoy. The justification of wars of

---

1   George M. Trevelyan, *Clio, A Muse, and Other Essays Literary and Pedestrian,* London, 1913, pp. 26–27.

self-defence is very convenient, since so far as I know there has never yet been a war which was not one of self-defence. Every strategist assures us that the true defence is offence; every great nation believes that its own overwhelming strength is the only possible guarantee of the world's peace and can only be secured by the defeat of other nations. In the present war, Serbia is defending itself against the brutal aggression of Austria-Hungary; Austria-Hungary is defending itself against the disruptive revolutionary agitation which Serbia is believed to have fomented; Russia is defending Slavdom against the menace of Teutonic aggression; Germany is defending Teutonic civilization against the encroachments of the Slav; France is defending itself against a repetition of 1870; and England, which sought only the preservation of the status quo, is defending itself against a prospective menace to its maritime supremacy. The claim of each side to be fighting in self-defence appears to the other side mere wanton hypocrisy, because in each case the other side believes that self-defence is only to be achieved by conquest. So long as the principle of self-defence is recognized as affording always a sufficient justification for war, this tragic conflict of irresistible claims remains unavoidable. In certain cases, where there is a clash of differing civilizations, a war of self-defence may be justified on the same grounds as a war of principle. I think, however, that, even as a matter of practical politics, the principle of non-resistance contains an immense measure of wisdom if only men would have the courage to carry it out. The evils suffered during a hostile invasion are suffered because resistance is offered: the Duchy of Luxemburg, which was not in a position to offer resistance, has escaped the fate of the other regions occupied by hostile troops. What one civilized nation can achieve against another by means of conquest is very much less than is commonly supposed. It is said, both here and in Germany, that each side is fighting for its existence; but when this phrase is scrutinized, it is found to cover a great deal of confusion of thought induced by unreasoning panic. We cannot destroy Germany even by a complete military victory, nor conversely, could Germany destroy England even if our Navy were sunk and London occupied by the Prussians. English civilization, the English language, English manufactures would still exist, and as a matter of practical politics it would be totally impossible for Germany to establish a tyranny in this country. If the Germans, instead of being resisted by force of arms, had been passively permitted to establish themselves wherever they pleased, the halo of glory and courage surrounding the brutality of military success would have been absent, and public opinion in Germany itself would have rendered any oppression impossible. The history of our own dealings with our colonies affords abundant examples to show that under such circumstances the refusal of self-government is not possible. In a word, it is the means of repelling hostile aggression which make hostile aggression disastrous and which generate the fear by which hostile nations come to think aggression justified. As between civilized nations, therefore, non-resistance would seem not only a distant religious ideal, but the course of practical wisdom. Only pride and fear stand in the way of its adoption. But the pride of military glory might be overcome by a nobler pride, and the fear might be overcome by a clearer realization of the solidity and indestructibility of a modern civilized nation.

## VI.

The last kind of war we have to consider is what I have called "the war of prestige." Prestige is seldom more than one element in the causes of a war, but it is often a very important element. In the present war, until the war had actually broken out, it was almost the only thing involved, although as soon as the war began other and much more important matters came to be at stake. The initial question between Austria and Russia was almost wholly one of prestige. The lives of Balkan peasants could not have been much affected for good or evil by the participation or non-participation of Austrian officials in the trial of supposed Serbian accomplices in the Sarajevo murders. This important question, which is the one on which the war is being fought, concerns what is called the hegemony of the Balkans, and this is entirely a question of prestige. Men desire the sense of triumph, and fear the sense of humiliation which they would have in yielding to the demands of another nation. Rather than forego the triumph, rather than endure the humiliation, they are willing to inflict upon the world all those disasters which it is now suffering and all that exhaustion and impoverishment which it must long continue to suffer. The willingness to inflict and endure such evils is almost universally praised; it is called high-spirited, worthy of a great nation, showing fidelity to ancestral traditions. The slightest sign of reasonableness is attributed to fear, and received with shame on the one side and with derision on the other. In private life exactly the same state of opinion existed so long as dueling was practiced, and exists still in those countries in which this custom still survives. It is now recognized, at any rate in the Anglo-Saxon world, that the so called "honor" which made dueling appear inevitable was a folly and a delusion. It is perhaps not too much to hope that the day may come when the honor of nations, like that of individuals, will be no longer measured by their willingness to inflict slaughter. It can hardly be hoped, however, that such a change will be brought about while the affairs of nations are left in the keeping of diplomatists whose status is bound up with the diplomatic or, military triumph of the countries from which they come, and whose manner of life renders them unusually ignorant of all the political and economic facts of real importance and of all the changes of opinions and organization which make the present world different from that of the eighteenth century. If any real progress is to be made in introducing sanity into international relations, it is vital that these relations should be in the hands of men less aloof and less aristocratic, more in touch with common life, and more emancipated from the prejudices of a bygone age. It is necessary also that popular education, instead of inflaming the hatred of foreigners and representing even the tiniest triumph as worthy of even the greatest sacrifices, should aim rather at producing some sense of the solidarity of mankind and of the paltriness of those objects to which diplomatists, often secretly, think fit to pledge the manhood and heroism of nations.

The objects for which men have fought in the past, whether just or unjust, are no longer to be achieved by wars amongst civilized nations. A great weight of tradition, of financial interests, of political insincerity, is bound up with the anachronism of international hostility. It is, however, perhaps not chimerical to hope that the present war, which has shocked the conscience of mankind more than any war in previous history, may produce a revulsion against antiquated methods, and may lead the exhausted nations to insist upon that brotherhood and co-operation which their rulers have hitherto denied them. There is no reason whatever against the settlement of all disputes by a Council of the Powers deliberating in public. Nothing stands in its way except the pride of rulers who wish to remain uncontrolled by anything higher than their own will. When this great tragedy has worked itself out to its disastrous conclusion, when the passions of hate and self-assertion have given place to compassion with the universal misery, the nations will perhaps realize that they have fought in blindness and delusion, and that the way of mercy is the way of happiness for all.

BERTRAND RUSSELL
*Trinity College, Cambridge*

# BIOGRAPHICAL TIMELINE

1872    Bertrand Arthur William Russell (3rd Earl Russell) is born on May 18 in Trellech, Monmouthshire, Wales, into an influential aristocratic family. He is the son of Viscount and Viscountess Amberley, who are radical for their time. His father, Lord Amberley, is known for his unorthodox views on religion and for his active support of birth control and women's suffrage, which contributed to the end of his short career as Liberal Member of Parliament. His mother, Lady Amberley, is a British suffragist and an early advocate of birth control in the United Kingdom. With her husband's consent, she has an affair with her children's tutor, the biologist Douglas Spalding. Russell is the godson of John Stuart Mill and the grandson of Lord John Russell (1st Earl), prime minister to Queen Victoria in the 1840s and 1860s. He has two siblings: a brother, Frank, who is seven years older and a sister, Rachel, who is four years older.

1874    Mother dies of diphtheria; sister Rachel's dies shortly thereafter.

1876    Father dies of bronchitis after a long depression. Russell, age four, and his older brother Frank move in with their rigidly Victorian grandparents (former Prime Minister Earl Russell and Countess Russell) in Richmond Park, London.

1883    Develops a passionate interest in mathematics after being introduced to Euclid by his brother Frank, an event that he describes in his autobiography as "one of the great events of my life, as dazzling as first love."

1887    Grandfather Lord John Russell dies, leaving the children entirely in the care of their grandmother, Countess Russell, a devout Scottish Presbyterian who successfully petitions the court to set aside a provision in Amberley's will requiring the children to be raised as agnostics. At this time, begins to doubt the validity of Christian religious dogma.

| | |
|---|---|
| 1889 | Meets future wife Alys Pearsall Smith, an American Quaker five years his elder and a graduate of Bryn Mawr College near Philadelphia. |
| 1890 | Becomes an atheist after reading Mill's *Autobiography*. |
| | Travels to European continent and visits the Eiffel Tower. |
| | Wins a scholarship to study mathematics at Trinity College, Cambridge. While at Cambridge, meets future co-author of *Principia Mathematica*, Alfred North Whitehead, and George Edward Moore, who would become a long-time collaborator. |
| 1893 | Graduates with a first-class B.A. in mathematics. |
| 1894 | Completes the Moral Sciences Tripos at Cambridge. |
| | Marries Alys Pearsall Smith on December 13. |
| 1896 | Publishes first work, *German Social Democracy*. |
| | Teaches German social democracy at the London School of Economics. |
| 1895 | Studies at the University of Berlin. |
| 1896 | Appointed lecturer at the London School of Economics; lectures in the US at Johns Hopkins and Bryn Mawr. |
| 1897 | *An Essay on the Foundations of Geometry*. |
| 1899 | Appointed lecturer at Trinity College, Cambridge. |
| 1900 | *A Critical Exposition of the Philosophy of Leibniz*. |
| | Attends the First International Congress of Philosophy in Paris and meets Giuseppe Peano whose *Formulario mathematico* is instrumental in his formulation of Russell's paradox, which he publishes the following year. |
| 1901 | Marriage to Alys Pearsall Smith begins to fall apart. |
| 1903 | Advances the famous paradox bearing his name in his work *The Principles of Mathematics*; publishes *A Free Man's Worship, and Other Essays*. |
| 1905 | Introduces the theory of descriptions in "On Denoting," which is published in the philosophical journal *Mind*. |

1907   Advocates, as a candidate for Parliament, for women's suffrage. Does not win election.

1908   Elected a Fellow of the Royal Society.

1910   *Philosophical Essays;* also publishes, with Alfred North Whitehead, the three-volume *Principia Mathematica* (1910–13).

Reappointed lecturer at Trinity College, Cambridge; is passed over for a Fellowship because of his "anti-clerical" views. Teaches and mentors Ludwig Wittgenstein.

1911   Separates from Alys Pearsall Smith; begins affair with Lady Ottoline Morrell, a society hostess and patron of writers such as Aldous Huxley, Siegfried Sassoon, T. S. Eliot, and D. H. Lawrence, and artists including Mark Gertler, Dora Carrington, and Gilbert Spencer. Also has simultaneous affairs with a number of other women, including, according to some, Vivienne Haigh-Wood, the English governess and writer, and first wife of T. S. Eliot.

1912   *The Problems of Philosophy.*

1913   Lectures at the École des Hautes Sociales in Paris.

1914   *Our Knowledge of the External World as a Field for Scientific Method in Philosophy.*

Visits Harvard and teaches courses in logic and the theory of knowledge; meets T. S. Eliot.

1916   *Principles of Social Reconstruction; Why Men Fight; Justice in War-time.*

Dismissed from Trinity College for passivist stance and agitating against British involvement in World War I, for which he is convicted under the Defence of the Realm Act 1914.

1917   *Political Ideals.*

Plays a significant part in the Leeds Convention in June, a gathering of well over a thousand "anti-war socialists." Including delegates from the Independent Labour Party and the Socialist Party, united in their pacifist beliefs and advocating a peace settlement.

1918      "The Philosophy of Logical Atomism" (a series of eight lectures); *Mysticism and Logic and Other Essays; Proposed Roads to Freedom: Socialism, Anarchism, and Syndicalism.*

Convicted and imprisoned for five months for lecturing against inviting the United States to enter the war on the United Kingdom's side.

1919      *Introduction to Mathematical Philosophy.*

1920      In January, Russell accepts offer of reinstatement at Trinity College due to pressure by majority of the Fellows of the College. However, requests a yearlong leave of absence. Over the summer, visits Soviet Russia as part of an official delegation sent by the British government to investigate the effects of the Russian Revolution. Meets Vladimir Lenin and, in his autobiography, writes that he found Lenin disappointing, sensing an "impish cruelty" in him. His first-hand experiences destroy his previous tentative support for the revolution.

Publishes *The Practice and Theory of Bolshevism* in November.

1921      *The Analysis of Mind.*

In January, resigns from Trinity College due to tumultuous events in his personal life.

Russell, accompanied by his lover Dora Black, a British author, feminist, and socialist campaigner, visits Peking (now Beijing) to lecture on philosophy.

On August 26, returns to England. Dora is six months pregnant. Hastily divorces Alys Pearsall Smith and marries Dora Black on September 27.

On November 16, Dora gives birth to John Conrad Russell, 4th Earl Russell.

1922      *The Problem of China;* "Free Thought and Official Propaganda" (lecture).

Knowing he is extremely unlikely to be elected in such a safe Conservative seat, unsuccessfully stands as a Labour Party candidate for Chelsea in the House of Commons.

1923     *The Prospects of Industrial Civilization* (with Dora Russell); *The ABC of Atoms.*

Again, unsuccessfully stands as a Labour Party candidate for Chelsea in the House of Commons.

Birth of daughter Katharine Jane Russell (later Lady Katharine Tait) on December 29.

1924     *Icarus; or, The Future of Science.*

1925     *The ABC of Relativity; What I Believe.*

1926     *On Education, Especially in Early Childhood.*

Delivers *Tarner Lectures* on the Philosophy of the Sciences at Trinity College.

1927     *The Analysis of Matter; An Outline of Philosophy;* "Why I Am Not a Christian" (lecture).

Co-founds the Beacon Hill School with his wife Dora Black.

1928     *Sceptical Essays.*

1929     *Marriage and Morals,* in which he advocates for equality between the sexes, no-fault divorce, expanded sexual and professional freedom for women, and other progressive social measures.

1930     *The Conquest of Happiness.*

Daughter Harriet Ruth is born on July 8.

1931     *The Scientific Outlook.*

Older brother Frank dies, thus becomes 3rd Earl Russell.

1932     *Education and the Social Order.*

Separates from Dora, who, during their marriage, had two children with American journalist, Griffin Barry.

Awarded the De Morgan Medal.

Becomes Chair of the India League, the foremost lobby in the United Kingdom for Indian independence, a position he holds until 1939.

1934     *Freedom and Organization, 1814–1914.*

Awarded the Sylvester Medal.

1935    *In Praise of Idleness and Other Essays; Religion and Science.*

Divorce from Dora.

1936    *Which Way to Peace?*

On January 18, marries third wife, Oxford undergraduate Patricia ("Peter") Spence, who had been his children's governess since 1930.

1937    Birth of son with Patricia Spence, Conrad Sebastian Robert Russell, 5th Earl Russell, who would become a prominent historian and one of the leading figures in the Liberal Democrat party.

Returns to London School of Economics to lecture on the science of power.

Opposes rearmament against Nazi Germany.

1938    *Power: A New Social Analysis.*

Appointed visiting professor of philosophy at Chicago.

1939    Appointed professor of philosophy at the University of California at Los Angeles.

1940    *An Inquiry into Meaning and Truth.*

Changes position on war with Germany and advocates defeating Hitler, who he believes poses a permanent threat to democracy in Europe.

Appointed professor at City College of New York. He is quickly dismissed, however, after a court judgment pronounces him "morally unfit" to teach at the college because of his opinions.

1941    Appointed lecturer at the Barnes Foundation in Pennsylvania.

1942    Dismissed from Barnes Foundation, but wins a lawsuit against the Foundation for wrongful dismissal.

1943    Expresses support for the creation of an Israeli state; adopts a stance toward warfare called "relative political pacifism" that holds that war, in extreme circumstances, may be the lesser of two evils.

1944    Reappointed Fellow at Trinity College.

1945     *A History of Western Philosophy; The Bomb and Civilisation.*

1948     *Human Knowledge: Its Scope and Limits.*

Is one of twenty-four survivors (among a total of forty-three passengers) of an airplane crash in Hommelvik, Norway, in October.

"Authority and the Individual" (series of six BBC broadcasts).

In a public speech at Westminster School, addressing a gathering arranged by the New Commonwealth, Russell shocks some observers by suggesting that a preemptive nuclear strike on the Soviet Union might be justified.

1949     *Authority and the Individual.*

Awarded the Order of Merit; elected a Lifetime Fellow at Trinity College.

1950     *Unpopular Essays.*

Awarded the Nobel Prize in Literature.

1951     *New Hopes for a Changing World.*

1952     *The Impact of Science on Society.*

Patricia Spence divorces Russell. On December 12, marries Edith Finch, an American writer and biographer, whom he had known since 1925.

1953     *Satan in the Suburbs and Other Stories.*

1954     *Human Society in Ethics and Politics; Nightmares of Eminent Persons and Other Stories.*

Delivers "Man's Peril" address on the BBC on December 23.

1955     Enlists Albert Einstein and numerous other luminary scientists to sign the Russell-Einstein Manifesto, which is issued on July 9. It highlights the dangers posed by nuclear weapons and calls for world leaders to seek peaceful resolutions to international conflict.

1956     *Portraits from Memory and Other Essays.*

Expresses opposition to European imperialism in the Middle East.

1957    Elected president of the first Pugwash Conference on Science and World Affairs, which drew its inspiration from the Russell-Einstein Manifesto of 1955.

1958    *Understanding History and Other Essays; The Will to Doubt.*

Founds the Campaign for Nuclear Disarmament.

1959    *Common Sense and Nuclear Warfare; My Philosophical Development.*

1961    *Fact and Fiction; Has Man a Future?*

At the age of eighty-nine, imprisoned for seven days for a "breach of the peace" after taking part in an anti-nuclear demonstration in London.

1963    *Essays in Skepticism; Unarmed Victory.*

Awarded the inaugural Jerusalem Prize; establishes the Bertrand Russell Peace Foundation.

1966    *The ABC of Relativity.*

1967    Launches the International War Crimes Tribunal.

Publishes *War Crimes in Vietnam* and a three-volume *Autobiography* beginning in 1967.

1970    On 31 January 1970, Russell issues a statement condemning "Israel's aggression in the Middle East," and in particular, Israeli bombing raids being carried out deep in Egyptian territory.

On February 2, Bertrand Russell dies of influenza in Penrhyndeudraeth, Wales, United Kingdom. His body is cremated in Colwyn Bay on February 5. In accordance with his will, there is no religious ceremony but one minute's silence; his ashes are later scattered over the Welsh mountains.

www.ingramcontent.com/pod-product-compliance
Lightning Source LLC
Chambersburg PA
CBHW032112280326
41933CB00009B/805